Other Schiffer Books on Related Subjects:

Jeans of the Old West, 2nd Edition, by Michael Harris, 978-0-7643-5263-8

Denim: An American Story, by David Little, 978-0-7643-2686-8

Motorcycle Jackets: A Century of Leather Design, 2nd Edition, by Rin Tanaka, 978-0-7643-2519-9

Library of Congress Control Number: 2018934126

Edited by Jesse J. Marth
Copyedited by Tod Benedict
Proofread by Kim Hufford
Cover and interiors designed by John P. Cheek
Cover photo by Joey Seawall (www.joeyseawall.com)
Type set in Din Pro / Futura Std

ISBN: 978-0-7643-5577-6
Printed in China

Published by Schiffer Fashion Press
An Imprint of Schiffer Publishing, Ltd.
4880 Lower Valley Road
Atglen, PA 19310
Phone: (610) 593-1777; Fax: (610) 593-2002
E-mail: Info@schifferbooks.com
Web: www.schifferbooks.com

For our complete selection of fine books on this and related subjects, please visit our website at www.schifferbooks.com. You may also write for a free catalog.

Schiffer Publishing's titles are available at special discounts for bulk purchases for sales promotions or premiums. Special editions, including personalized covers, corporate imprints, and excerpts, can be created in large quantities for special needs. For more information, contact the publisher.

We are always looking for people to write books on new and related subjects. If you have an idea for a book, please contact us at proposals@schifferbooks.com.

Our book is dedicated with much love to our dear parents,
Tony and Barbara Williams,
Vicente and Flordeliza Corpuz,
and to our beautiful boy, Elijah (Eli)

We would like to thank Andrew Olah, Emily Olah, and the Kingpins team for their support in making this book.

www.kingpinsshow.com

KINGPINS SHOW ♛

also thanks to
Tracey Panek, historian
at Levi Strauss and Co., San Francisco, California.

Jean Svadlenak, Nancy White & Bobbie Hamzioui,
at Lee® Jeans, Merriam, Kansas.

Craig Errington, VP of marketing
at VF Jeanswear, Greensboro, North Carolina.

Evan Morrison and Joey Seawell for working with us at the
Wrangler archive and on all other photography taken in
Greensboro, North Carolina.

Jesse Marth, Pete Schiffer, and all at
Schiffer Publishing, Ltd.

CONTENTS

FOREWORD

When Levi Strauss & Co. and tailor J. W. Davis patented the idea for riveted pockets in 1873, they had little inkling that their creation—the world's first blue jeans—would become a global phenomenon. Today, denim is worn all over the planet by people of all ages and backgrounds. Fans of denim and blue jeans everywhere will appreciate Nick Williams's *Denim Branded* and his efforts to lay out the design details of the evolution of blue jeans from their workwear beginnings. Nick provides a one-source guide to comparing denim brands with enough detail to date garments or to recognize a manufacturer. Nick's clear text makes *Denim Branded* an easy-to-use denim reference for anyone hoping to understand how differences in sundries—from rivets to buttons—as well as design create distinct brand characteristics.

–Tracey Panek, Levi Strauss & Co. historian

INTRODUCTION

From the first Diesel sample sale that I attended around 1992 (when I moved to New York from London to work as a print textile designer), my interest in denim branding was born. The labels and tags attached to the clothing caught my attention because they had a vintage Americana aesthetic. The clothing range was called Old Glory and took inspiration from the big-three denim brands: Levi Strauss & Co., Wrangler, and Lee® Jeans.

There have been many other influences and experiences that have contributed to my passion for denim branding, including my time at Levi Strauss & Co. Europe. One of the jobs that I enjoyed the most was re-creating the branding artwork from some of their archived vintage pieces, which would have originally been created using machinery, into digital format so that it could be used on the Levis® Vintage Clothing (LVC) range. This involved visiting the Levi Strauss & Co. archive in San Francisco. I would carefully study every branding element to ensure that the re-created artwork would be historically accurate. The detailed process and experience of working hands-on with such a historical archive was educational and immensely impressionable. I also gained an appreciation and understanding of heritage and authenticity, which are extremely hard to execute in a genuine and believable way.

This is, in part, one of the reasons for creating this book. I wanted to create an inspirational source or reference that was exclusively dedicated to denim branding. As a graphic designer, I have accumulated a library of reference books (many published by Schiffer) over the years, which have inspired me and continue to be of great use, but I have always wished for a book that specialized in denim branding. With the encouragement of my wife and business partner, Jenny, we got the ball rolling.

We share an affinity for Americana, so it was a natural collaboration for us to work on (with our three-year-old son, Eli, in tow). Creating the book started out as a passion project with a clear mission of creating a useful reference that was heavily weighted with inspirational imagery. But the path in which we were led opened up opportunities that were beyond my wildest dreams.

The first was being given consent by the big-three denim brands not only to feature them in our book but to be given access to their archives. This led us to San Francisco, California; Merriam, Kansas; and Greensboro, North Carolina. Seeing and experiencing their archives was such a thrill and honor, but one of the most memorable experiences was visiting Cone Mill's White Oak Plant in Greensboro. I can still hear and feel the strong rhythmic beat of the original wooden Draper looms working proudly and tenaciously weaving the beautiful American selvage denim. At the time we did not realize it would be only months later that the plant would announce its closure.

Denim has such a rich history, and every branding element on a piece of denim has a story behind it. Each of the brands featured in the book has generously helped us tell some of that story by revealing part of their own. I am so very humbled with the amazing brands and contributors who have made this book possible. Some are instigators, inspirers, and groundbreakers, but all share passion, dedication, talent, and respect for one of the most beloved pieces of apparel.

What started off as a passion project has turned into an homage to all the brands and people who have and continue to be involved in the world of denim. My passion and appreciation goes beyond denim branding, but never more so after having experienced the journey of creating this book.

THE RIVET

Rivet on 'XX' denim waist overalls, c. 1879
Courtesy of Levi Strauss & Co. Archives

Jacob Youphes was born in 1831 near Riga, Latvia. He was a trained tailor when he emigrated from the Russian Empire to the New World in 1854, aged 23. He landed in New York, where he worked as a journeyman tailor. Jacob changed his name to Jacob Davis and went by the name J. W. Determined to seek his fortune elsewhere, J. W. made the monthlong sea voyage in 1856 to the city built by fortune hunters, San Francisco. However, he did not settle in San Francisco at this time. Instead he traveled around the West and ventured into several businesses, including a brewery, coal, and tobacco, none of them resulting in a great fortune. With the development of the railroad, new opportunities in a new town were in sight. In 1868, J. W. took his growing family to Reno. After another failed brewery business, he returned to his craft and opened a tailoring shop on Virginia Street. However, here his craft was more suited to the demands of the working men of Reno. They needed items such as horse blankets, tents, and wagon covers made from off-white duck cloth, which was purchased from Levi Strauss & Co.

One day in 1870, Jacob's lack of fortune took a pivot when the wife of a laborer came into the shop and asked him to make a pair of inexpensive pants that could withstand the strenuous workload of a laborer and his rather large frame. Davis crafted the pants from heavy, ten-ounce cotton duck twill that was likely purchased from Levi Strauss & Co, since he was a customer. Upon finishing the pants, Davis decided to reinforce the corners of the front and rear pockets by hammering in the copper rivets that he used on the horse blankets. A logical decision by Davis, but one that would change his status from tailor to entrepreneur. As the months went by, Davis started to accumulate orders from miners, teamsters, and surveyors, all demanding his increasingly popular riveted pants. Over the next couple of years, Davis realized his calling and more importantly his customers'. By this time he was using his rivets on blue fabric, likely denim. Demand was starting to outweigh his capacity to produce, and he knew that soon enough his competitors would start catching onto his design. Davis needed to patent his design, and he needed to find a way to distribute his product on a mass scale. Who better to approach than the company that had been with him on this journey all along, Levi Strauss & Co. He wrote to Levi Strauss about the success and continued high demand for his riveted pants. He proposed that they jointly apply for a patent, explaining that his riveted overalls were selling at a premium price of $3.00 a pair. Davis offered Levi Strauss exclusive sales in the Pacific states and territories, and the remaining United States and half of the Pacific coast would be J. W.'s. On April 26, 1873, Davis moved his family to San Francisco, having been invited by Levi Strauss to oversee the manufacture of the riveted pants. On May 20, 1873, after a few amendments and revisions of the patent application, it was finally granted in the names of Jacob Davis and Levi Strauss & Co., of San Francisco, California.

Rivets on prewash New Nevada 1880s watch pocket
Courtesy of Levi Strauss & Co. Archives

Rivets removed from watch pocket for the duration of World War II
Courtesy of Levi Strauss & Co. Archives

This date is proudly branded on the rivet, as well as the company's initials. Under the new Levi Strauss & Co. and Davis partnership, the humble rivet was still hammered into the pants by seamstresses in their homes. Demand grew and production evolved until the flat-head-hammered rivet eventually became attached by machine, resulting in the now-round-head nipple rivet.

As ingenious and important as the rivet is, the new protruding rivet caused some problems. Consumers complained about the rivets scratching saddles, car seats, and furniture. In the 1930s, Levi Strauss & Co. hid the rivet under fabric on the back pockets. Reassuring consumers that the rivets still existed, they created the pocket "flasher" (more on that to come). However, the hidden, back-pocket rivets were permanently removed in the 1960s, since they inevitably wore through the fabric.

World War II meant rationing, and Levi Strauss & Co.'s overalls were not an exception. Due to the conservation of metal and material requirements, Levi Strauss & Co. removed the rivets from the small pocket on the right-hand side of their overalls, referred to as the watch pocket by Levi Strauss & Co. (also referred to as the match pocket or coin pocket, depending on whom you ask), as well as the rivet at the base of the button fly. After the war, the small pocket rivets were reinstated. Not so for the "crotch" rivet. Levi Strauss & Co. received mounting complaints from cowboys who, when sitting close to campfires, experienced the discomfort of a heated rivet! The crotch rivet was removed permanently when the then president of Levi Strauss & Co., Walter Haas Sr., himself experienced such discomfort during a camping trip.

Around 1890, Levi Strauss & Co.'s patent for riveted clothes expired, allowing other companies to use rivets on their clothing.

The H. D. Lee® Mercantile Company (a successful independent wholesale grocery distributor established in 1889) started making garments in 1912 and by the 1920s used rivets on garments such as the 101 Cowboy denim pant. In 1936 the back pocket rivet was replaced by Lee®'s reinforcing-stitch technique, the "bartack." One of Lee®'s most famous signatures.

Wrangler jeans designed the more refined "flat rivet" in 1947, which proudly advertised its benefit of being "no scratch."

Rivets have remained a staple of denim. Initially an integral element used to reinforce stress points of pocket corners, they have now evolved into a decorative logo statement by denim brands such as King of Indigo's (K.O.I) koi carp, DENHAM the Jeanmaker's tailor scissors, and Butcher of Blue's Butcher hook logo. More recently, Italian denim mill Candiani created the "golden rivet" (*Rivetto D'Oro* in Italian). Entrusted to only a select few jeans makers worldwide, the rivet is Candiani's seal of premium quality and is used only on their finest Italian denim.

Lee® watch pocket rivet, 1960–1970
Courtesy of Lee® Jeans / Photographer Bobbie Hamzioui

Lee® center back cinch rivet, 1938. These pants likely were made in 1938—after Lee® removed rivets from back pockets. The rivets seen in the photo on the back cinch belt may have been used between 1924 and 1935.
Courtesy of Lee® Jeans / Photographer Bobbie Hamzioui

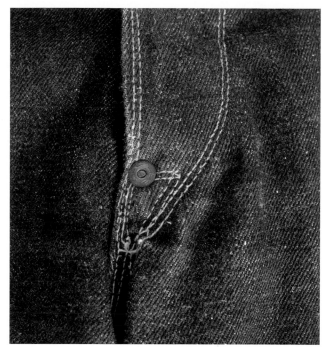

Boss of the Road pocket rivet, 1920–1939. Boss of the Road was an Eloesser-Heynemann product before the company was purchased by Lee® in 1946.
Courtesy of Lee® Jeans / Photographer Bobbie Hamzioui

Lee® crotch rivet on hair-on-hide patch waist overalls, 1938–1945. The hair-on-hide waistband patch was used from 1938 to 1945.
Courtesy of Lee® Jeans / Photographer Bobbie Hamzioui

Lee® center back cinch rivet on hair-on-hide patch waist overalls, 1938–1945
Courtesy of Lee® Jeans / Photographer Bobbie Hamzioui

Lee® back pocket bartack on hair-on-hide patch waist overalls, 1938–1945
Courtesy of Lee® Jeans / Photographer Bobbie Hamzioui

1940s 11MW prototype-era Blue Bell's Wrangler Jeans with signature Rodeo Ben coin pocket
Courtesy of Wrangler Archive / Photographer Joey Seawell

1960s 13MWZ steel rivet with copper finish
Courtesy of Wrangler Archive / Photographer Joey Seawell

1950s Blue Bell Jeanies "UFO" rivet with domed-cap steel rivet with copper finish
Courtesy of Wrangler Archive / Photographer Joey Seawell

Sugar Cane & Co. rivets, 2016
Courtesy of photographer Shuhei Nomachi / TOYO Enterprise Co., Ltd.

Sugar Cane & Co. rivets, 2016
Courtesy of photographer Shuhei Nomachi / TOYO Enterprise Co., Ltd.

Eat Dust match pocket rivets, c. 2017
Courtesy of Eat Dust /
Photographer Thomas Skou

Eat Dust skull logo rivet back, c. 2017
Courtesy of Eat Dust /
Photographer Thomas Skou

Endrime rivet
Courtesy of Endrime

The design concept of the sundries for ENDRIME was based on Arabic square "Kufic" text. Kufic is one of the oldest calligraphic forms and its modified form of the older Naba-taean script. Logos designed in square Kufic are considered a very hard task—and often revered. I decided early on to use my first name, Mohsin, on all of the buttons and rivets in Kufic, but I took it further by applying it into a circular form to fit the sundries.

—Mohsin Sajid, Endrime

18

Kings of Indigo rivet, c. 2017
Courtesy of Kings of Indigo

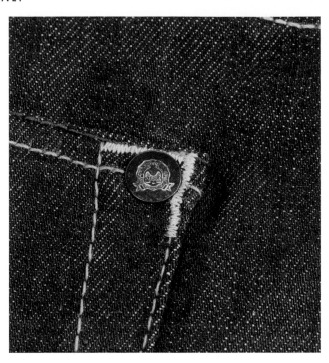

Koi Carp logo rivet, c. 2017
Courtesy of Kings of Indigo

Works Inc. rivet, 2017
Courtesy of Sam Poole, Iron Heart International Ltd.

Embossed pure-copper rivets, c. 2017
Courtesy of Ali Kirby & Catharina Veder at
DENHAM the Jeanmaker

Black-powder-coated nipple rivet with pure copper nail, c. 2017
Courtesy of Ali Kirby & Catharina Veder at
DENHAM the Jeanmaker

Rivetto D'Oro, "The Golden Rivet." The Candiani Denim mark of Italian craftsmanship, c. 2017.
Courtesy of Ali Kirby & Catharina Veder at
DENHAM the Jeanmaker

Leather rivet saddles to increase durability and comfort, c. 2017
Courtesy of Ali Kirby & Catharina Veder at
DENHAM the Jeanmaker

Butcher Hook logo rivet, c. 2017
Courtesy of Butcher of Blue

Rivet back, c. 2017
Courtesy of Butcher of Blue

Evisu hidden rivet
Courtesy of Evisu Group Limited

Evisu match pocket rivet
Courtesy of Evisu Group Limited

Match pocket rivets
Courtesy of Christian McCann, Left Field NYC

Skull logo on back of rivets
Courtesy of Christian McCann, Left Field NYC

The Skull head we use as one of our logos was brought in when I first started the brand and wanted to use a separate label for outlaw culture, biker, latino gangster, criminals, and other derelicts; the label I was using at the time was a varsity style, a baseball diamond, and it just didn't makes sense, so we used the skull head to represent the new direction, and it is incorporated on all the backs of the tacks on our jeans.

–Christian McCann, Left Field NYC

BUTTONS

Scovill Fasteners salesman sample display card, c. 1920s
Courtesy of Scovill Fasteners

A prolific button manufacturer, Scovill Fasteners, is another heritage brand with a rich history. When the United States was only twenty-six years old, a small button-making shop that would become Scovill Fasteners was founded in Waterbury, Connecticut, in 1802. Since the company's inception they have been a part of military history by developing the United States' first gilt buttons. Uniforms for US Army soldiers and US Navy sailors in the War of 1812 were adorned with Scovill Fasteners' pewter shank buttons. In 1825, Scovill Fasteners crafted seventeen solid-gold closures featuring the head of George Washington as a gift to General Marquis de Lafayette (the last surviving general of the Revolutionary War) on his visit to the US. A key contributor of branded product developments since the beginning of the denim industry, Scovill Fasteners was one of the very first button suppliers to the forefather denim companies. Over many decades, Scovill Fasteners has been the leading button supplier to companies such as Sweet Orr, Lee®, Wrangler, and Carhartt. Throughout the World War years, Scovill Fasteners' operations ran twenty-four hours a day to manufacture and deliver billions of metal components to the allies for their armaments needs.

Scovill Fasteners salesman sample display card, c. 1920s
Courtesy of Scovill Fasteners

Scovill Fasteners salesman sample display card, c. 1920s
Courtesy of Scovill Fasteners

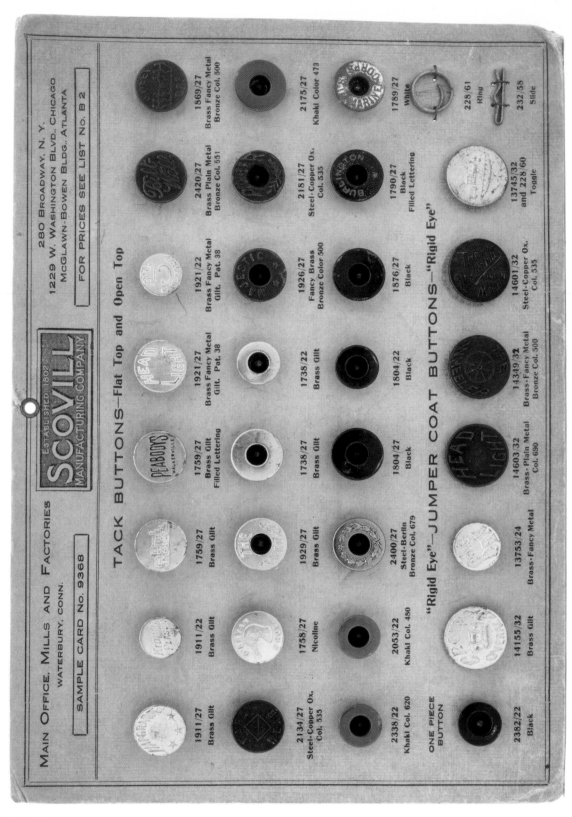

Scovill Fasteners salesman sample display card, c. 1920s
Courtesy of Scovill Fasteners

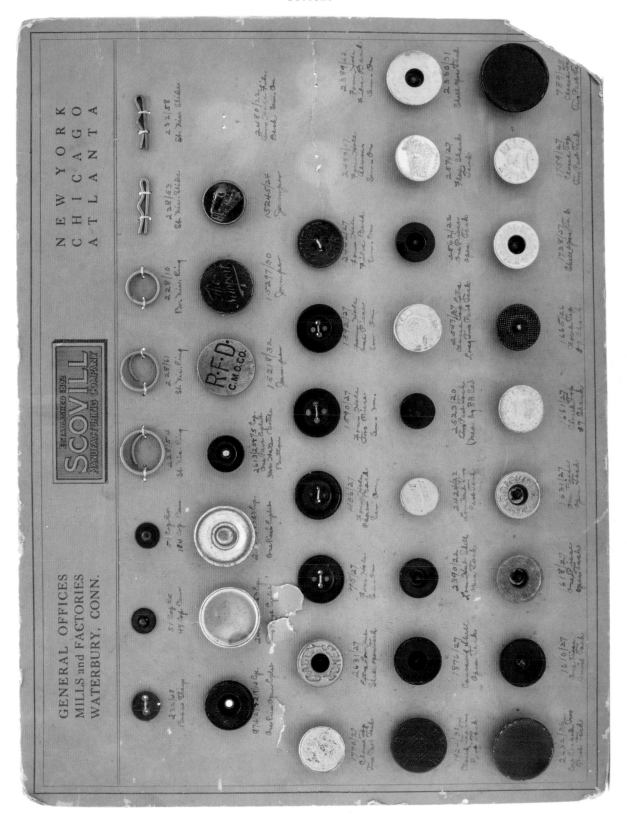

Scovill Fasteners salesman sample display card, c. 1920s
Courtesy of Scovill Fasteners

The first Levi Strauss & Co. overalls would have had sewn-on buttons as opposed to shank-style buttons, such as the ones on the beautifully preserved New Nevada Jean, which is dated around 1880. There is no branding on these buttons, and it is not certain when the first branded Levi Strauss & Co. button was created. The button has experienced a lot of design changes through the years. From 1902 to 1928, a black button was generally used on the more economical 201 series; apart from LVC reproduction pieces, the black button was used only on this line during this period. The infill has been removed and reinstated and "SF CAL" was stamped alongside "Levi Strauss & Co." More significantly, during World War II the iconic Levi Strauss & Co. surround branding on buttons was generally replaced with a standard laurel leaf (thought to have represented peace) or was unbranded. President Franklin D. Roosevelt established the World Production Agency (WPA), a government agency that set standards for manufacturers in order to ration materials during the wartime period. This included metal and cotton.

Waist band button on prewash New Nevada, 1880s
Courtesy of Levi Strauss & Co. Archives

Fly button on denim waist overalls, c. 1879
Courtesy of Levi Strauss & Co. Archives

Laurel wreath button used during WWII
Courtesy of Levi Strauss & Co. Archives

Top fly button on "Spur Bites" overalls, 1890
Courtesy of Levi Strauss & Co. Archives

Boss of the Road waistband "donut" button, on Boss of the Road waistband overalls, 1920–1939. Boss of the Road—Eloesser-Heynemann product before the company was purchased by Lee® in 1946.
Courtesy of Lee® Jeans / Photographer Bobbie Hamzioui

Can't Bust' Em button on Can't Bust' Em overalls, 1940–1949. Though Lee® purchased Eloesser-Heynemann in 1946, E-H continued to manufacture Cant Bust' Em products after 1946.
Courtesy of Lee® Jeans / Photographer Bobbie Hamzioui

Lee® wreath logo button on Lee® Jelt denim overalls, 1939–1945. This round, black, doughnut-style button features a wreath of leaves like one used in labels from the 1890s for H. D. Lee® Mercantile products. The doughnut button was used during WWII in response to the metal shortages from the intense demand for metal for war equipment and armaments. This button is believed to have been used exclusively during WWII.
Courtesy of Lee® Jeans / Photographer Bobbie Hamzioui

Long "L" Lee® logo pocket snap on Lee® Jelt Denim overalls, snap: 1931–1945. Though the the Long "L" log was introduced before 1919, Jelt Denim was introduced in 1931.
Courtesy of Lee® Jeans / Photographer Bobbie Hamzioui

Lee® Riders waistband button on Lee® 101
Riders, 1949–1959
Courtesy of Lee® Jeans / Photographer Bobbie Hamzioui

Lee® Cowboy "donut" button on Lee® 101
Cowboy Overalls waistband, button: 1925-1947, pants: 1938
Courtesy of Lee® Jeans / Photographer Bobbie Hamzioui

Union Made by Lee® "donut" button on Lee® 101 Cowboy
Pants, 1960–1970
Courtesy of Lee® Jeans / Photographer Bobbie Hamzioui

Tall "e" Lee® logo button on Lee® painters overalls, 1960–1970
Courtesy of Lee® Jeans / Photographer Bobbie Hamzioui

Lee® Riders 101 button-front Cowboy Pants, 1946–1955
Courtesy of Lee® Jeans / Photographer Bobbie Hamzioui

Long "L" Lee® logo button on Lee® 101J Jacket. This jacket was made between 1936 and 1939; buttons used as early as 1919 (or earlier)
Courtesy of Lee® Jeans /
Photographer Bobbie Hamzioui

Union Made by Lee® pocket snap on Lee® 101J Jacket. This jacket was made between 1931 and 1939; Union-Made snaps, 1931–1942
Courtesy of Lee® Jeans /
Photographer Bobbie Hamzioui

Lee® 91J Jacket: This jacket was made between 1936 and 1939; buttons used as early as 1919 (or earlier). "Long L" logo button—1919–1962 (possibly earlier). When this logo was registered with the US Patent Office in 1929, it had reportedly been used as early as 1919 and continued to be used until it was generally replaced by the "tall E" Lee® logo button, introduced around 1960. The long "L" may have been used even earlier than 1919; however, no records have been found to know for sure what logo Lee® used on its earliest workwear. This long "L" logo button was used in tandem with the "Union-All," "Union-Made by Lee®," WWII buttons, and "tall E" introduced in 1960–61. However, the long "L" appears in print ads in 1962.
Courtesy of Lee® Jeans / Photographer Bobbie Hamzioui

1950s 111MJ keyhole buttonhole and Scovill Fasteners
Wrangler steel tack button with copper finished cap
Courtesy of Wrangler Archive / Photographer Joey Seawell

1980s No Fault Denims Wrangler Tack Button with Antiqued Copper Finish
Courtesy of Wrangler Archive / Photographer Joey Seawell

1980s Wrangler 13MWZ tack button with copper finish
Courtesy of Wrangler Archive / Photographer Joey Seawell

1960s Wrangler Women's jean tack button with nickel finish and red-enamel-painted Wrangler roped logo
Courtesy of Wrangler Archive / Photographer Joey Seawell

1970s Wrangler limited-edition print twill jeans with Scovill Fasteners Gripper® Snap Fastener in nickel finish with red-enamel-painted Wrangler roped logo
Courtesy of Wrangler Archive / Photographer Joey Seawell

1970s Lady Wrangler Scovill Fasteners Gripper® Snap Fastener with red-enamel-painted Lady Wrangler roped logo
Courtesy of Wrangler Archive / Photographer Joey Seawell

1960s Wrangler pinto wash jeans with tack button with nickel finish and red-enamel-painted roped logo
Courtesy of Wrangler Archive / Photographer Joey Seawell

888MJL flannel-lined, pleated-front jacket internal placket showing domed steel shank for tack buttons, with factory stamping "C-8" identifying manufacture origin within Blue Bell's family of factories. Also, the 8 oz. left-hand twill selvage is exposed, showing the selvage of the fabric used to terminate the placket of the jacket pattern.
Courtesy of Wrangler Archive / Photographer Joey Seawell

1940s Blue Bell overalls in new old stock with keyhole buttonhole, red bartack, and Blue Bell Scovill Fasteners tack button
Courtesy of Wrangler Archive / Photographer Joey Seawell

1950s Sanforized Scovill Fasteners Gripper® Snap Fastener in brass finish
Courtesy of Wrangler Archive / Photographer Joey Seawell

1970s-made reproduction 1930 Blue Bell overalls in pincheck with donut button with nipple fastener and cinch prong overall hanger
Courtesy of Wrangler Archive / Photographer Joey Seawell

1950s Blue Bell Scovill Fasteners Gripper® Snap Fastener tack button in copper finish
Courtesy of Wrangler Archive / Photographer Joey Seawell

1950s Blue Gem Overall Company (Greensboro, NC) Scovill Fasteners Gripper® Snap Fastener tack button in brass finish with blue-enamel-paint fill
Courtesy of the Morrison Collection / Photographer Joey Seawell

1950s Belk's Red Camel overalls (Charlotte, NC) Scovill Fasteners Gripper® Snap Fastener tack button in brass finish with red-enamel-paint fill
Courtesy of the Morrison Collection / Photographer Joey Seawell

1930s US Army zinc four-eye button for M1937 denim popover utility work shirt and pants, issued both to US Army and Civilian Conservation Corps prior to World War II during the National Recovery Act
Courtesy of the Morrison Collection / Photographer Joey Seawell

1920s texturized-steel four-eye button painted in black enamel with whirl pattern
Courtesy of the Morrison Collection / Photographer Joey Seawell

1930s Casey Jones big 8 oz. Sanforized cone deeptone denim work dungaree with double-button waistband and signature Casey Jones train button in patina copper finish.
Courtesy of the Morrison Collection /
Photographer Joey Seawell

1940s laurel wreath one-star button with black enamel finish, issued generically during WWII to domestic manufacturers
Courtesy of the Morrison Collection /
Photographer Joey Seawell

1930s J. C. Penney Co. Super Pay Day 8 oz. overall tack button with nickel finish and red enamel paint.
Parva-brand slide overall hanger fastener.
Courtesy of the Morrison Collection / Photographer Joey Seawell

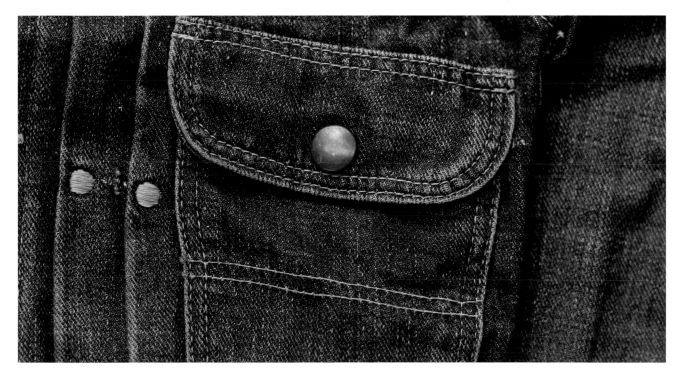

1950s 8BJ Blue Bell Wrangler blank Scovill Fasteners Gripper® Snap Fastener with copper finish
Courtesy of Wrangler Archive / Photographer Joey Seawell

Details of 66MW Blue Bell Wrangler shirt with sulfuric black vat-dyed denim shirting called "Midnight Black," diamond-shaped Scovill Fasteners Gripper® Snap Fastener pearl snaps, and post-1955 tilted-bell Blue Bell Wrangler woven label
Courtesy of Wrangler Archive / Photographer Joey Seawell

1950s second-edition Blue Bell Wrangler 27MW shirt with Scovill Fasteners Gripper® Snap Fasteners with white-enamel-paint fill, slant pockets, and western-style sleeve placket and throat. Wrangler woven label.
Courtesy of Wrangler Archive / Photographer Joey Seawell

40

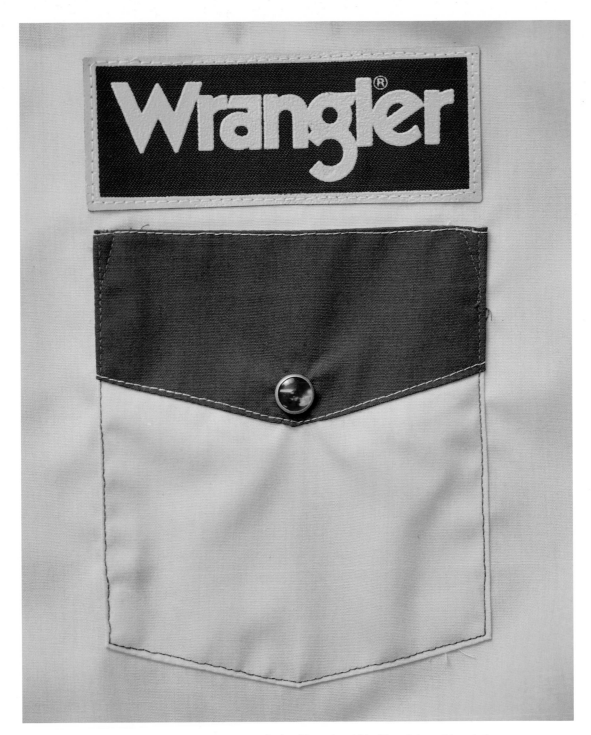

1980s Dale Earnhardt Sr. Nascar Endorsement Series Wrangler shirt with patch and jeweled
Scovill Fasteners Gripper® Snap Fastener
Courtesy of Wrangler Archive / Photographer Joey Seawell

1950s first edition Blue Bell Wrangler 27MW shirt with Scovill Fasteners Gripper® Snap Fasteners in brushed nickel finish, pre-1955 vertical-bell Blue Bell Wrangler woven label, and hand repairs
Courtesy of the Morrison Collection / Photographer Joey Seawell

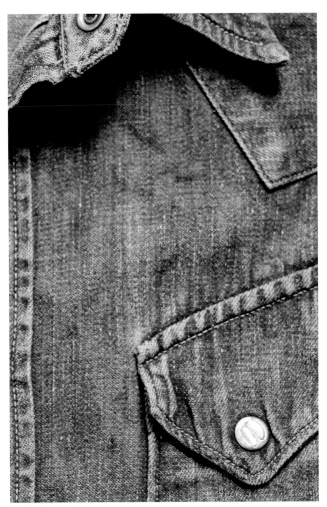

Details of 1950s first-edition Blue Bell Wrangler 27MW shirt with Scovill Fasteners Gripper® Snap Fasteners in brushed-nickel finish, pre-1955 vertical-bell Blue Bell Wrangler woven label, and hand repairs
Courtesy of the Morrison Collection / Photographer Joey Seawell

1960s Blue Bell Wrangler 24MJZL; detail of copper button with roped Wrangler logo and Troy Woolen Mills Troyset blanket lining
Courtesy of Wrangler Archive / Photographer Joey Seawell.

1950s Blue Bell Wrangler 8BJL prototype boy's three-pocket, blanket-lined jacket; detail of blank copper buttons, straight-line pocket stitching and welt pocket
Courtesy of Wrangler Archive / Photographer Joey Seawell

1920s Red Arrow overall button in brass tack style, fastened to sling-back overall, produced by High Point Overall Company of High Point, North Carolina, also makers of Anvil Brand Overalls. Overalls made of 2x1 RHT 8 oz. denim.
Courtesy of the Morrison Collection /
Photographer Joey Seawell

1950s Blue Bell overalls model 8MS 8 oz. Overalls in denim, Blue Bell logo, and Scovill Fasteners button in brass finish
Courtesy of Wrangler Archive / Photographer Joey Seawell

Round House and Ben Davis Co. dungaree button. Ben Davis Manufacturing was founded in 1935 by Simon Davis and his son Benjamin Franklin Davis, the grandson of Jacob W. Davis, co-creator of the first riveted blue jean with Levi Strauss & Co. Round House workwear was founded in Oklahoma in 1903 and was a favorite among railroad workers. It is the oldest operating denim jeans and overalls manufacturing company in Oklahoma.
Author's collection

46

Sugar Cane & Co. buttons, 2016
Courtesy of photographer Shuhei Nomachi / TOYO Enterprise Co., Ltd.

Sugar Cane & Co. Buttons, 2016
Courtesy of photographer Shuhei Nomachi / TOYO Enterprise Co., Ltd.

Diesel Buttons, c. 1992
Courtesy of Wouter Munnichs, founder of Long John *online magazine*

Diesel Buttons, c. 1992
Courtesy of Wouter Munnichs, founder of Long John

Compilation image of Carhartt buttons, top to bottom, left to right: 1889, 1900, 1905, 1910, 1910, 1915
Courtesy of the Carhartt Archive

Compilation image of Carhartt buttons, top to bottom, left to right: 1920, 1920, 1925, 1940, 1940, 1989
Courtesy of the Carhartt Archive

Waistline button, c. 2017
Courtesy of Eat Dust / Photographer Thomas Skou

Jacket button, c. 2017
*Courtesy of Eat Dust /
Photographer Thomas Skou*

Snap button, c. 2017
*Courtesy of Eat Dust /
Photographer Thomas Skou*

Rogue Territory feather logo donut button, c. 2017
Courtesy of Rogue Territory LLC

Evisu waistline button, c. 2016
Courtesy of Evisu Group Limited

Donut button, c. 2016
Courtesy of Dawson Denim

Cheesehead screw-inspired logo button, c. 2016
Courtesy of Dawson Denim

Waistline button, 2017
Courtesy of Sam Poole, Iron Heart International Ltd.

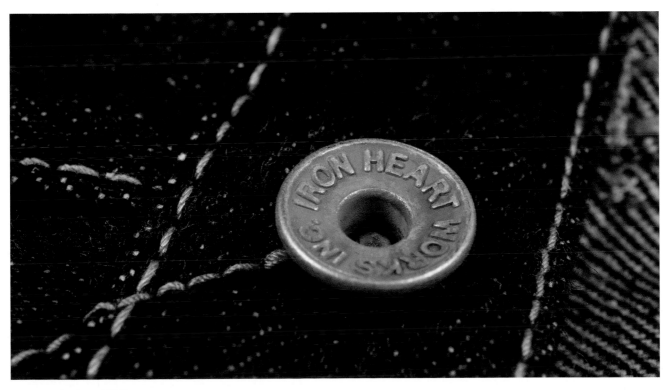

Waistline button, 2017
Courtesy of Sam Poole, Iron Heart International Ltd.

Buttons and rivets
Courtesy of Endrime

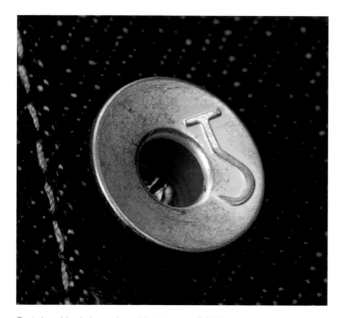

Butcher Hook logo donut button, c. 2017
Courtesy of Butcher of Blue

Butcher Hook logo donut button, c. 2017
Courtesy of Butcher of Blue

Recycled copper donut button, blackened steel shank, c. 2017
Courtesy of Ali Kirby & Catharina Veder at DENHAM the Jeanmaker

Blue watercolor varnish, copper shank, c. 2017
Courtesy of Ali Kirby & Catharina Veder at DENHAM the Jeanmaker

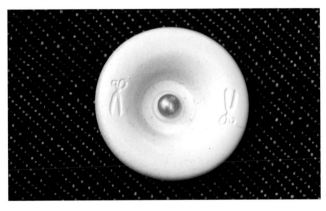

Powder-sprayed in BMW car plant, c. 2017
Courtesy of Ali Kirby & Catharina Veder at DENHAM the Jeanmaker

Hand-red Japanese copper, c. 2017
Courtesy of Ali Kirby & Catharina Veder at DENHAM the Jeanmaker

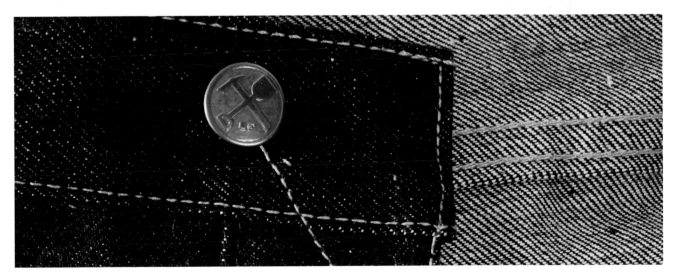

Coal miner pick-and-shovel tack button
Courtesy of Christian McCann, Left Field NYC

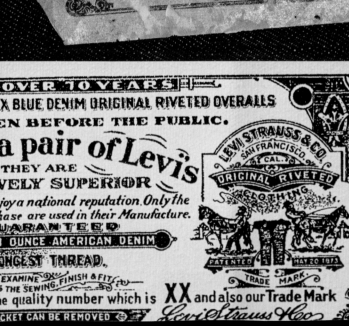

GUARANTEE TICKET

First featured on Levi Strauss & Co.'s denim pants around 1892, the guarantee ticket is possibly the first graphic label featured on the exterior of any overalls. Originally made from oil cloth, it was sewn onto the back pocket. It was not only a confirmation of authenticity, it also noted the garment's fit, size, fabric and overall quality, strength, and awards. Prior to this, these features were printed on the inside of the pocket bag. After the patent expired on the rivets in 1890 (LS&Co. may have reapplied for it), Levi Strauss & Co, decided to create a label containing this information, to be attached to the outside of the pants so that they would stand out on the shelf of the local store. The original guarantee ticket had "This is a pair of them" written on it. By the mid-1920s, it came to the attention of Levi Strauss & Co. that the word "Levi's" had become the generic name for any pair of riveted denim pants that had started to flood the market from competitors. In order to protect and authenticate their original and premium product, they applied for a new trademark in 1927 with the name "Levi's." The trademark was registered in 1928, and the guarantee ticket was redesigned that year to read "This is a pair of Levi's."

The guarantee ticket has continued to be redesigned over the years, with notable changes. You will notice that the years at the top of the ticket will have increased with the company's age.

It is of course printed on paper now instead of oil cloth. The graphics on the oldest guarantee ticket known are refined and dense with information. Over the years the content of the ticket has evolved and the size has changed, some being smaller. Color was introduced to highlight features of the pants but also to proudly display the LEVI'S® brand name within the iconic red-rectangle-tab shape.

Being such a revolutionary piece of denim branding, many denim brands have, of course, paid homage to it. The guarantee ticket to me is one of the most important denim-branding elements because it is the beginning of graphic design on a detachable label, which was the predecessor of the pocket flasher and the hangtag, which is where my fascination with denim branding began.

Guarantee ticket on deadstock 1953 501®
Courtesy of Levi Strauss & Co. Archives

Guarantee ticket on deadstock 1966 501®
Courtesy of Levi Strauss & Co. Archives

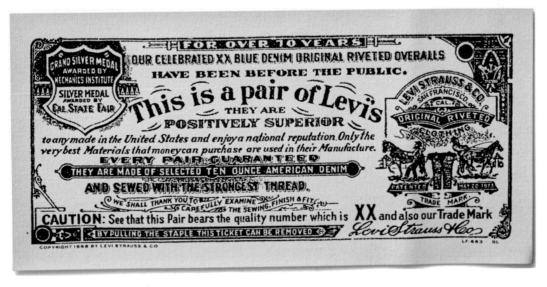

Compilation photo of reproduction guarantee tickets used on Levi's® Vintage Clothing
Author's collection / Photographer Joey Seawell

Only Genuine
Lee® OVERALLS
Have All These Features!

| Jelt Denim | Genuine Korn Stripes | 2-Ply Side Reinforcement | Union Made | Lee Tailored Sizes | 4-in-1 Bib Pocket |

Look for the
UNION LABEL
on this Garment

| tch Pocket | Slot Lock Loops | Can't Creep Slides | Rust-Proofed Buttons | Form Fitting Bib | Shield Back |

| Crotch | Hidden Seams | Triple Seams | Cordea Buttonholes | Serged Fly | Save-Loss Pocket |

| om Pockets | Lined Hip Pockets | Interwoven Suspenders | Thread Riveted | Match Pocket | Rule & Pliers Pockets |

GUARANTEE
This Lee Overall must look better, fit better

SANFORIZED
Fabric Shrinkage Not More Than 1%
(Standard Test CS 59-36)

WASHINGTON
TRADE MARK   REG.U.S.PAT.OFF.

"DEE·CEE"
THE FINISHED OVERALL
OR LONG COMFORTABLE SERVICE
· SANFORIZED ·

GRADUATED FOR BETTER FIT
· GUARANTEED ·

10 oz.
(36" Width)
INDIGO BLUE
DENIM

GARMENT IS CUT OVER A PATTERN PROPORTIONED TO FIT
U ASSURES PERFECT COMFORT AND IS FULLY GUARANTEED.
YOUR DEALER WILL REFUND YOUR MONEY
IF NOT SATISFACTORY

IRON HEART
EXTRA HEAVY DENIM
21

JEANS & DENIM WE
ORIGINAL GARME
MY FAVORITE RUGGED WE
ESSENTIAL OF U.S.A. CLOTHI

Men's Bib Overall

8 oz

· SANFORIZED ·
FABRIC SHRINKAGE LESS THAN 1%

Guaranteed by
Good Housekeeping

BLUE BELL

Qualitag   TRADE MARK

BLUE BELL'S GUARANTEE TO YOU

PAPER LABELS

The guarantee ticket was one of the first oil cloth labels on denim pants. Oil cloth would later be replaced by paper. From 1912 until 1937, brands such as Lee® and Blue Bell Overall Company had paper labeling on their coveralls, overalls, and dungarees. These labels advertised and informed the consumer of the durability and high-quality features of the garment.

One of the most key branding pieces that has become synonymous and unique to jeanswear is the pocket flasher. Bluebell designed large, graphic paper labels on their "Big Ben" overalls, as did other brands, but Levi Strauss & Co.'s "bat wing" shape is probably the most iconic. Designed to gain the consumer's attention and to inform them that their favorite denim pants now carried "concealed copper rivets" (having been hidden due to scratch issues), the label contained the famous phrase "the rivet's still there." This phrase was used as a strap line in marketing and advertising. For the duration of WWII the wording on the LS&Co. pocket flasher was changed. It noted that the article complied in every way with requirements of the War Production Board (WPB). The overall design of the Levi's pocket flasher is so timeless and classic that it has become a staple part of branding a jean. Some brands have and still do pay homage to the Levi Strauss & Co. pocket flasher in great detail, from the shape of the label to the content.

Bluebell created the "Qualitag," a little booklet that contained information about the garment. It was first used in 1944 and copyrighted in 1945. When Bluebell transitioned into "Wrangler," the booklet was titled *Great Moments in Rodeo*. It capitalized on the popularity of comics during that time and contained a comic strip about rodeo riders that appealed both to the western market and kids.

Lee® created the "Whizit" and "Blue Ribbon" labels, which were directly sewn onto the garment. The "Blue Ribbon" logo was reminiscent of first-prize ribbons won in rodeos and fairs. Lee® also used paper pocket flashers on their pants beginning in the 1940s.

It is not only denim retail brands that have been able to convey the quality of their garments, but denim mills have been co-branding with denim brands since the mid-twentieth century. One of the oldest mills still in existence, Cone Mills in Greensboro, North Carolina, has been co-branding with countless denim brands (too many to mention) and still continue to do so. Some brands include Wrangler, Levi Strauss & Co., Blue Buckle, and J. C. Penney. Italian denim mill Candiani's premium denim produced for DENHAM the Jeanmaker is highlighted not only by their "Golden Rivet" but also the special hangtag noting the all-important sustainability and innovation of the fabric.

Denim paper labels come in all shapes and sizes. Workwear labels are typically larger to clearly illustrate the benefits of the garment to the consumer, whereas the pocket flasher is generally smaller in size and fits neatly into the back pocket. Brands such as Wrangler, Lee®, and Maverick brought the spirit of their brands to life with vibrant color and illustrations. It would be impossible to fit all of the amazing labels that we found, and it was certainly a tough job whittling the number down. In the same vein as the guarantee ticket, which made Levi's® overalls stand out in the local shop, a lot of the paper labels from the mid- to late twentieth century were designed in the same spirit. They initially captured the consumer's eye with pop colors and playful illustrations while informing them of the garment's assets. Among the sea of indigo, these labels really drew a customer in. Now, denim brands have a wealth of historical references regarding denim branding and there is a wonderful mix of minimalist and vintage design. Reputed modern small-batch brands such as Endrime and Dawson Denim have a more modern, simplistic design to their pocket flasher and hangtag, letting the craftsmanship of their jean shine through. Brands such as Sugar Cane, Kings of Indigo, and Iron Heart create an authentic heritage feel in their paper labels. DENHAM the Jeanmaker cleverly conveys to the consumer the thought and craftsmanship behind their jeans through the shape of their labels. Their back-pocket plaster illustrates that the seven-point design of their back pocket is perfectly shaped for the natural anatomy of the hand, and their custom hangtag mirrors the pattern cutting of a pair of jeans.

The mid-twentieth century was, graphically, the golden era of paper labels. The rich color, hand-drawn illustrations, and printing process resulted in the pieces of artwork we revere today. What is more amazing is that these types of labels would be produced only in small runs today for limited-edition pieces or small-batch producers due to cost. Back in the day, these were produced in volume!

No matter how detailed or minimalist a paper label design is, the spirit of the denim brand should always be at its core.

Pocket flasher on deadstock 1953 501® *Courtesy of Levi Strauss & Co. Archives*

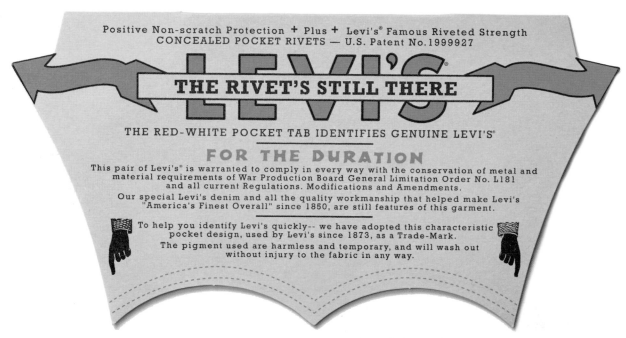

Reproduction wartime guarantee tickets used on Levi's® Vintage Clothing
Author's collection / Photographer Joey Seawell

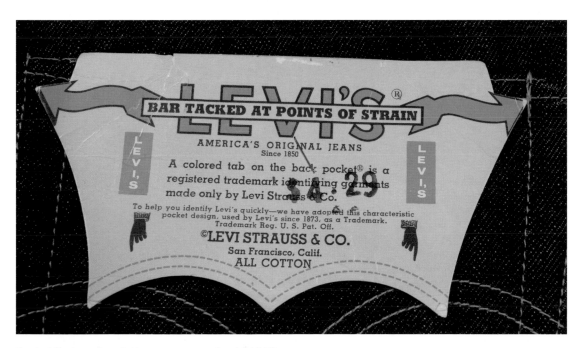

Pocket flasher after rivets were removed, mid-1960s
Courtesy of Levi Strauss & Co. Archives

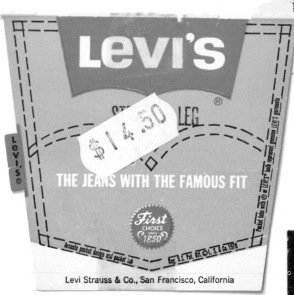

1970s Levi's® pocket flasher
Author's collection / Photographer Joey Seawell

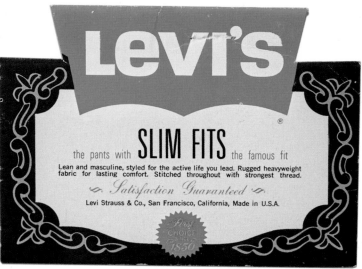

Reproduction 1970s Slim Fits pocket flasher
used on Levi's® Vintage Clothing
Author's collection / Photographer Joey Seawell

Reproduction 1960s pocket flasher used on
Levi's® Vintage Clothing
Author's collection / Photographer Joey Seawell

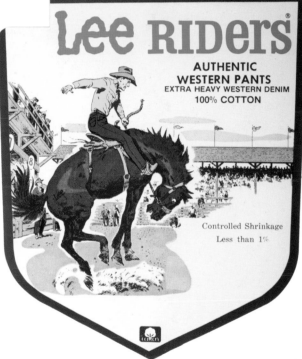

Lee® product label (pocket flasher): Lee® Riders Authentic Western Pants (bucking-bronco label), first used in 1948. Lee® first used this graphic on product labels in 1948, and it has been used frequently since then. Trademark registered in 1969. This example dates from after 1969, when Lee® was purchased by Vanity Fair (a division of VF Corporation). *Courtesy of Lee® Jeans*

Lee® product label (pocket flasher): Lee® Westerner, Lee® PReST, trademark registered / first use in 1964. *Courtesy of Lee® Jeans*

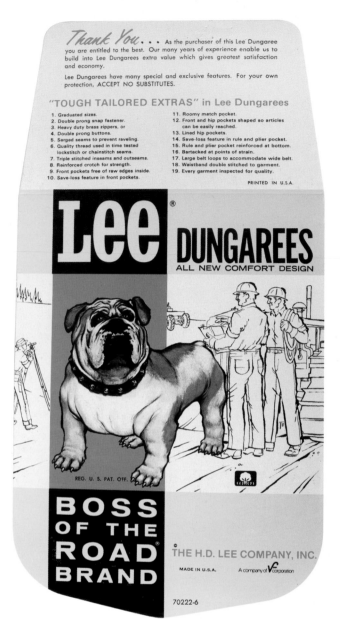

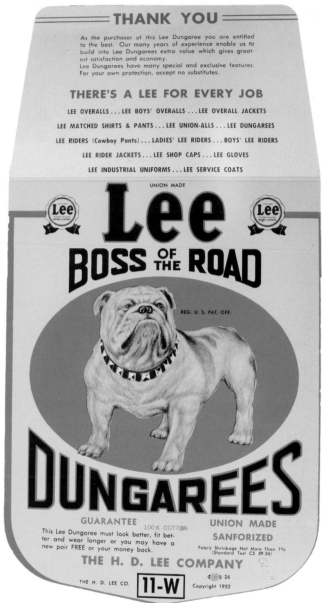

Lee® product label (pocket flasher): Lee® Boss of the Road Dungarees, 1970–1975. Eloesser-Heynemann Company of San Francisco first owned the trademark for Boss of the Road. Lee® purchased E-H in 1946 and Lee® was purchased by VF in 1969. See at bottom of flasher: "A company of VF Corporation."
Courtesy of Lee® Jeans

Lee® product label (pocket flasher): Lee® Boss of the Road Dungarees, 1952. This label was first used in 1952 (copyrighted by Lee® in 1953) and was used for many years after.
Courtesy of Lee® Jeans

Lee® product label (pocket flasher): Lee® overalls, 1949. This label was copyrighted by Lee® in 1949 and was used for many years after.
Courtesy of Lee® Jeans / Photographer Bobbie Hamzioui

Lee® product label: Lee® overalls, 1931–1939. Lee® began including "Sanforized-Shrunk" on labeling in 1936. Salina, Kansas, is listed as the location where this pair was made. Since that factory closed in 1947, these must have been made before that year. This version of Lee®'s "Blue Ribbon" on the paper label dates from approximately 1931–1939.
Courtesy of Lee® Jeans / Photographer Bobbie Hamzioui

Lee® product label: Lee® Whizit overall, 1927–1939
Courtesy of Lee® Jeans / Photographer Bobbie Hamzioui

74255-19

77's AND 88's **RUGGED**
ROOMY CUT FOR COMFORT AND EASY ACTION

STURDY 14 OZ. COARSE-WEAVE DENIM

COPPER RIVETED FOR LONGER WEAR

CHOICE OF BUTTONS OR ZIPPER

BOSS OF THE ROAD®

LEE COMPANY
A company of VF corporation

Lee®

MADE IN U.S.A.

Lee® product label: Lee® Boss of the Road 77s and 88s, 1970–1980. "VF" on label—post-1969
Courtesy of Lee® Jeans

MADE IN U.S.A.
THE H. D. LEE COMPANY INC.
A company of VF corporation
70852-6

Lee™
K.C. BLUES
COLLECTION
FOR GALS AND GUYS

"The Fit to Be Tried"

Lee® product label: Lee® K.C. Blues Collection, 1975–1976. Shown/listed in January 1976 catalog. Lee® registered for the "K.C. BLUES" trademark on April 26, 1977 (filed application April 25, 1975; first use March 17, 1975).
Courtesy of Lee® Jeans

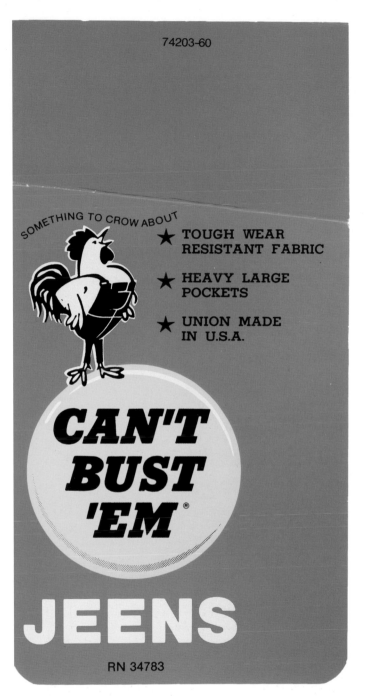

Can't Bust 'Em Jeens, c. 1974
Courtesy of Lee® Jeans

Can't Bust 'Em Work Clothes, 1958. The Eloesser-Heynemann Company, which Lee® bought in 1946, created Can't Bust 'Ems. *Courtesy of Lee® Jeans*

**USE THIS CHART AS YOUR
SIZE GUIDE TO ASSURE
CORRECT FIT AND REAL COMFORT**

SIZE	4	5	6	7	8	9	10	11	12	13	14	15	16	18
WAIST														
SLIM	19½	20	20½	21	21½	22	22½	23	23½	24	24½	25	25½	26½
REGULAR	21½	22	22½	23	23½	24	24½	25	26	26½	27	27½	28½	
INSEAM														
SLIM-REG.	17	18½	20½	21½	23	24½	25½	26½	28	29½	30½	31	32½	

PRINTED IN U.S.A.

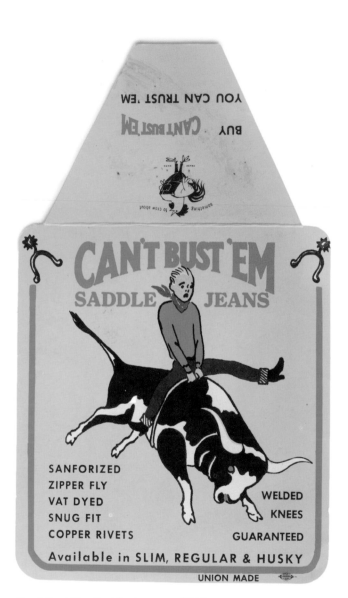

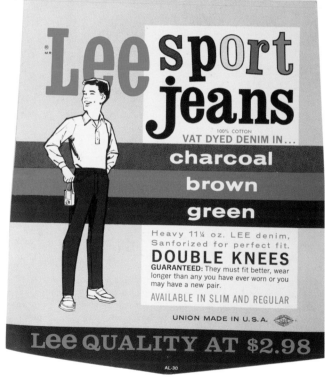

Can't Bust 'Em Saddle Jeans, c. 1940
Courtesy of Lee® Jeans

Lee® product label: Lee® Sport Jeans (for boys), 1963–1970. The Lee® (RMR) logo indicates this tag was made sometime after 1962, when Lee® began to use labels with the "MR" in compliance with laws in Mexico (where the use of the MR was compulsory), and when Lee® started to sell garments in Mexico and Latin America. However, some Lee® products made as early as 1958 show the RMR symbols.
Courtesy of Lee® Jeans

Can't Bust 'Em Western Style Saddle Jeans, c. 1945
Courtesy of Lee® Jeans

Lee® product label (pocket flasher): Lee® Hipster Jeans, 1960–1968. This flasher includes the "Big E" Lee® logo of the 1960s. The appearance of the "racol" after the Lee® name also indicates this was after 1960 since it does not include "a company of VF Corporation," which was added in 1970. "Racol" was likely used before 1969, when VF acquired Lee®.
Courtesy of Lee® Jeans

A Special Label Honoring the Cowboy's Turtle Association

"Fearless Riders of the Rodeo Arena"

Rodeo—the only sport originating in a major industry—cattle raising. Early days, at big round-ups, Cowboys from neighboring ranches would match their skill. But now Rodeo is a major sport—next to baseball as a National pastime. In no other sport is competition so keen, yet bonds of comradeship so binding. Great credit is due "The Cowboy's Turtle Association", more than 1200 men risking their necks for glory, for popularizing famous traditions of American Frontier life. A Turtle Show is Rodeo at its Best.

UNION MADE

Lee

11½ OZ. DENIM. *SANFORIZED SHRUNK

COWBOY PANTS

Approved by the Cowboy's Turtle Association
"Lee Cowboy Pants More Than Meet Our Standards"
* Fabric Shrinkage Less Than 1%—Standard Test CS-59-36

The H. D. Lee Merc. Company

SAN FRANCISCO, CALIF. • KANSAS CITY, MO. • SALINA, KANS.
MINNEAPOLIS, MINN. • SOUTH BEND, IND. • TRENTON, N. J.

COPYRIGHT 1940
THE H. D. LEE
MERC. CO.

Lee® Cowboy Pants, special label honoring the Cowboy Turtle Association, 1940
Courtesy of Lee® Jeans

74

1950s pocket flasher on Blue Bell overalls Model 8MS 8 oz. overalls in denim
Courtesy of Wrangler Archive / Photographer Joey Seawell

LOOK WELL IN BLUE BELL

BLUE BELL

- **8 oz. DENIM**

Extra heavy, extra rugged. They are •SANFORIZED• Fabric shrinkage less than 1%. Buy your exact size.

- **GUARANTEED**

The best made, best fitting you can buy — or your money back!

Please See Other Side

REPLACEMENT OR REFUND OF MONEY
Guaranteed by
Good Housekeeping
IF NOT AS ADVERTISED THEREIN

BLUE BELL
GREENSBORO, NORTH CAROLINA

LOT 8 MS

1950s Qualitag on Blue Bell overalls model 8MS 8 oz. in denim with generic "Sanforized" script and Scovill Fasteners tack button in brass finish
Courtesy of Wrangler Archive / Photographer Joey Seawell

PAPER LABELS

1980s Wrangler staple-fastened paper labels with roped logo and singular wrangler branding
Courtesy of Wrangler Archive / Photographer Joey Seawell

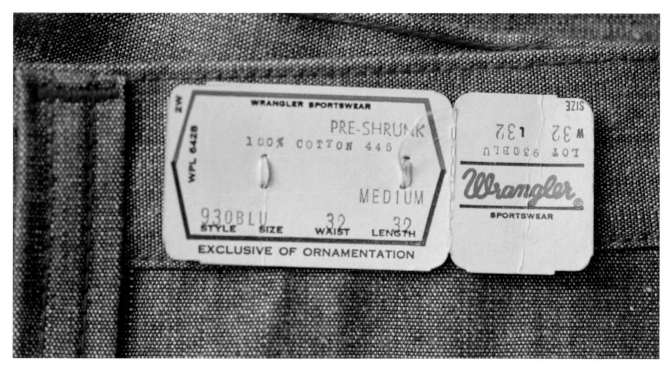

1970s Wrangler Sportswear sew-on label containing model and lot information
Courtesy of Wrangler Archive / Photographer Joey Seawell

Mid-1950s Blue Bell Jeanies side-zip jeans in new old stock with paper flashers, labels, and rat tail tags, pre-1955
Courtesy of Wrangler Archive / Photographer Joey Seawell

78

Early 1950s Blue Bell Jeanies Qualitag, the signature informational flasher that was tagged to Blue Bell clothing beginning in the early 1950s
Courtesy of Wrangler Archive / Photographer Joey Seawell

1970s Wrangler flasher artwork on Flare Leg Jeans
Courtesy of Wrangler Archive / Photographer Joey Seawell

PAPER LABELS

Guaranteed
If this garment should prove defective in any way return it directly to us for replacement or refund at our option.

LOW CUT
WASHABLE

Wrangler ®

FLARES

Hecho en Honduras por FABRICA BOLIVAR bajo licencia de
Blue Bell, Inc., Greensboro, N.C. U.S.A.

1950s private label flasher artwork for Alexander's by Blue Bell
Courtesy of Wrangler Archive /
Photographer Joey Seawell

STYLED BY BLUE BELL EXPRESSLY FOR

ALEXANDER'S

Ⓐ WESTERN JEANS

13¾ OZ. DENIM
•SANFORIZED•
FABRIC SHRINKAGE LESS THAN 1%

- **NARROW LEGS**
  Form fitting
- **NO-SCRATCH COPPER RIVETS**
  At all points of strain
- **JAM PROOF ZIPPER CLOSURE**

MADE IN U.S.A.

M 25

NO BETTER GARMENT MADE

RED CAMEL
QUALITY WORK CLOTHES

SATISFACTION GUARANTEED

- Sanforized
- Double Stitched, Strong, Roomy Pockets
- All Points of Strain Reinforced
- Non-Rip Seams Neatly Sewed
- Tailored to Fit
- Quality Materials, Vat-Dyed

A CERTIFIED Ⓑ BETTER VALUE

Built for STRENGTH and ENDURANCE

— **SALESPEOPLE** —
Detach from garment when sold.
SAVE THIS STUB
for making up order for fill-in sizes

LOT **55TZ**   SIZE   PRICE

1950s vat-dyed twill work pants pocket flasher for button attachment by Belk's Red Camel for lot 55TZ
Courtesy of Wrangler Archive /
Photographer Joey Seawell

1980s Wrangler pocket flasher artwork with Cotton logo and silent "W" advertising
Courtesy of Wrangler Archive / Photographer Joey Seawell

8 OUNCE SANFORIZED MAXIMUM SHRINKAGE 1%

BLUE BELL

Lot No. 13 BH

Manufactured by Blue Bell, Inc.

WORLD'S LARGEST PRODUCER OF WORK CLOTHES

GENERAL SALES OFFICES, 93 WORTH ST., NEW YORK 13, N.Y.

Guaranteed by Good Housekeeping

Size 16 · BB ★ 8 OUNCE · Sanforized · Buy Exact Size for Perfect Fit · Size 16

1940s Blue Bell overalls 8 oz. in new old stock with
paper pocket flasher artwork in cyanic blue and paper
size label inset into pocket
*Courtesy of Wrangler Archive /
Photographer Joey Seawell*

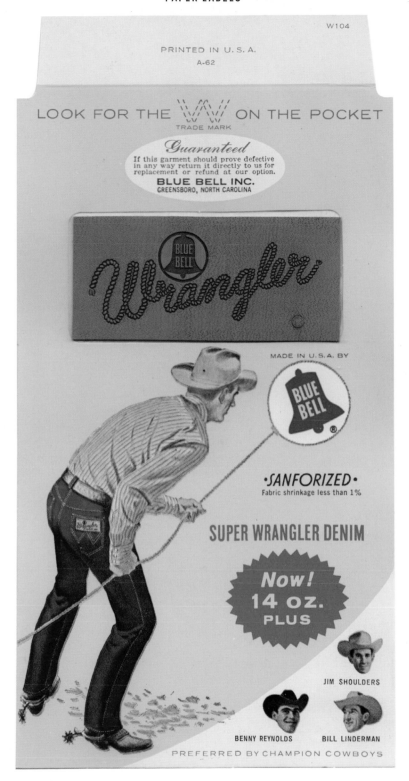

Early 1950s men's western denim pocket flasher sample with neolite Blue Bell Wrangler (pre-1955) label inset for sampling. Note that the 14 oz. likely dates these between 1953 and 1955.
Courtesy of Wrangler Archive / Photographer Joey Seawell

1950s–1970s examples of pocket flasher artwork for Blue Bell, Wrangler, Blue Bell Wrangler, Blue Bell Maverick, and Big Lee®d clothing
Courtesy of Wrangler Archive / Photographer Joey Seawell

Retro-inspired flasher artwork from 1980s to 2010s for Wrangler products
Courtesy of Wrangler Archive / Photographer Joey Seawell

1940s Blue Buckle Young Bill junior overalls lot 30B in new old stock with paper pocket flasher and paper inset size label, co-branded with Cone deeptone denim, first launched in 1936
Courtesy of the Morrison Collection / Photographer Joey Seawell

1940s Big Favorite overalls in new old stock made by the Favorite Garment
Company of Lynchburg, Virginia, made in 8 oz. Sanforized denim lot 4154B
Courtesy of the Morrison Collection / Photographer Joey Seawell

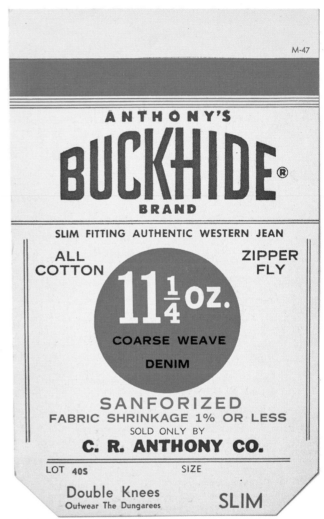

1950s C. R. Anthony Buckhide brand flasher artwork, a
private label produced by Blue Bell Inc. for a department
store, lots 95Y and 40S
Courtesy of Wrangler Archive / Photographer Joey Seawell

1950s Casey Jones by Blue Bell pocket flasher for work dungarees lot 8MDZ in 10 oz. denim
Courtesy of Wrangler Archive / Photographer Joey Seawell

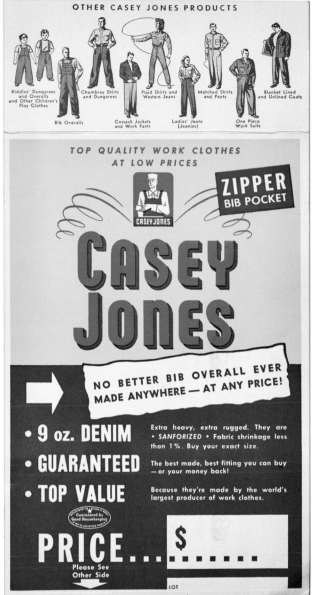

1950s Casey Jones by Blue Bell pocket flasher for 9 oz. zipper bib overalls
Courtesy of Wrangler Archive / Photographer Joey Seawell

1950s Blue Bell for boys' cargo pocket jeans button flasher (inspired by World War II clothing designs for uniforms) (pre-1955)
Courtesy of Wrangler Archive / Photographer Joey Seawell

91

1940s overalls paper pocket flasher artwork examples for Big 30 (private label by Blue Bell) and the Big Favorite (the Favorite Garment Company)
Courtesy of Wrangler Archive / Photographer Joey Seawell

1950s private label by Blue Bell Powder Horn and Bar 9
western jeans paper pocket flasher artwork, jam-proof zipper
Courtesy of Wrangler Archive / Photographer Joey Seawell

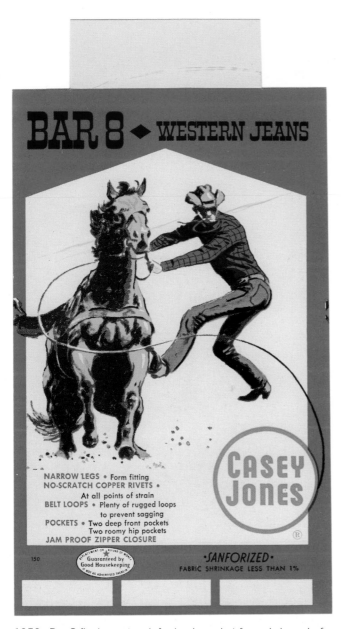

1950s Bar 8 flasher artwork for back pocket for sub-brand of Blue Bell
Courtesy of Wrangler Archive / Photographer Joey Seawell

1970s Peter Max for Wrangler artwork, rat tail flasher tag
Courtesy of the Morrison Collection / Photographer Joey Seawell

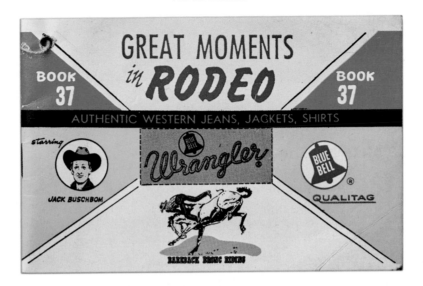

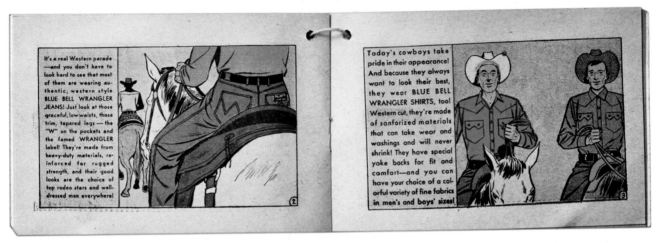

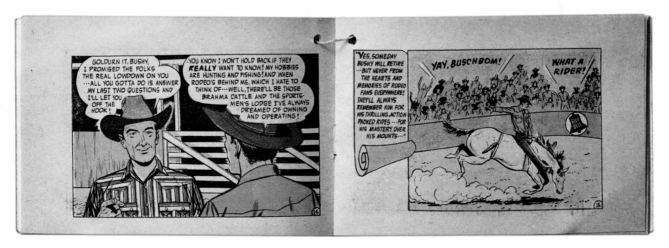

Blue Bell Wrangler post-1955 *Great Moments in Rodeo* cartoon rat tail tag included as Qualitag of information and novelty with purchase of Blue Bell Wrangler jeans, book 37, starring cowboy legend Jack Buschbom
Author's collection / Photographer Joey Seawell

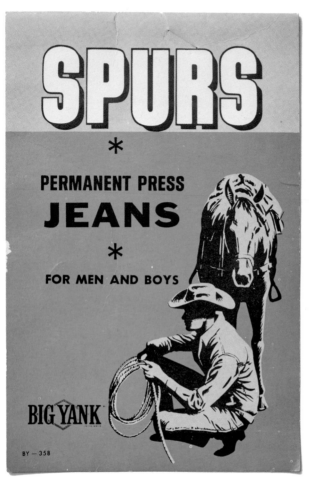

Big Yank product label, date unknown
Author's collection / Photographer Joey Seawell

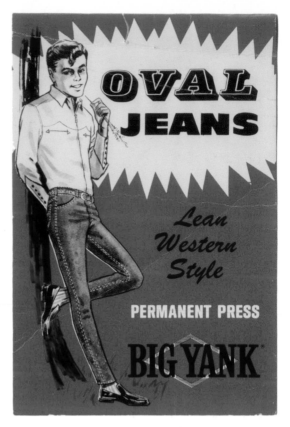

Big Yank product label, date unknown
Author's collection / Photographer Joey Seawell

Saddle King product label, date unknown
Author's collection / Photographer Joey Seawell

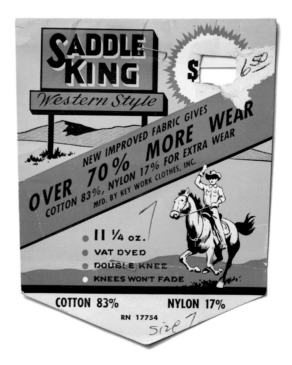

Carhartt product label, date unknown
Courtesy of the Carhartt Archive

Carhartt product label, date unknown
Courtesy of the Carhartt Archive

Carhartt product label, date unknown
Courtesy of the Carhartt Archive

Diesel paper product label, c. 1992
*Author's collection /
Photographer Joey Seawell*

Diesel paper product label, c. 1992
*Author's collection /
Photographer Joey Seawell*

Diesel paper product labels, c. 1992
Author's collection / Photographer Joey Seawell

Sugar Cane & Co. product label, 2016
Courtesy of photographer Shuhei Nomachi / TOYO Enterprise Co., Ltd.

Sugar Cane & Co. product label, 2016
Courtesy of photographer Shuhei Nomachi / TOYO Enterprise Co., Ltd.

Sugar Cane & Co. product label, 2016
Courtesy of photographer Shuhei Nomachi / TOYO Enterprise Co., Ltd.

Kings of Indigo paper pocket flasher, c. 2017
Courtesy of Kings of Indigo

Kings of Indigo Kids Koi paper pocket flasher, c. 2017
Courtesy of Kings of Indigo

Paper pocket flasher, c. 2017
Courtesy of Sam Poole, Iron Heart International Ltd.

Paper pocket flasher, c. 2017
Courtesy of Sam Poole, Iron Heart International Ltd.

Deadstock Washington Dee Cee Sanforized 10 oz. denim overalls, c. 1960
Author's collection

Dawson Denim paper pocket flasher with typeface designed specifically for the British railway network in the 1920s
Courtesy of Dawson Denim

Dawson Denim log book inspired by founder Scott Ogden's grandfather's driving license from the 1930s, which acts as a repair service manual
Courtesy of Dawson Denim

Endrime pocket flasher
Courtesy of Endrime

[The] pocket flasher was developed after the first prototype jean was finalized. The pocket flasher is a pencil sketch drawing of the pocket design—down to every stitch—and perfectly mirrors the pocket shape underneath.
The video-game-inspired ENDRIME logo, together with the complete Kufic circle "MOHSIN SAJID" stamp, are joined with Japanese katakana text under the main logo. There is also a thank-you message on the flap that's hidden.

–Mohsin Sajid, Endrime

Back-pocket plaster: The seven-point pocket fits the natural anatomy of the hand.
Courtesy of Ali Kirby & Catharina Veder at DENHAM the Jeanmaker

Custom hangtag: Gloss-coated front, spot UV lettering, and unbleached backside white card
Courtesy of Ali Kirby & Catharina Veder at DENHAM the Jeanmaker

PAPER LABELS

FSC heavy-stock card, high-frequency matt-gloss-overprinted logo hangtag
Courtesy of Ali Kirby & Catharina Veder at DENHAM the Jeanmaker

Candiani Italian premium fabric identity hangtag promoting sustainability and innovation in fabrication
Courtesy of Ali Kirby & Catharina Veder at DENHAM the Jeanmaker

Left Field paper pocket flashers, letterpress hand stamped
Courtesy of Christian McCann, Left Field NYC

Opposite page:
Stack of BLKSMTH Denim at Loren
Manufacturing Inc., Brooklyn, New York
Courtesy of Loren Cronk /
Photography by Martin Scott Powell

WOVEN LABELS

Big "E" Red Tab on dead stock waist overalls, 1937
Courtesy of Levi Strauss & Co. Archives.

Without a doubt, the most famous woven label in the denim world is Levi Strauss & Co.'s "Red Tab Device" (as it is legally called). The iconic piece of denim branding was recommended back in 1936 by national sales manager Chris Lucier. Due to the rise in competitors' jeans after the patent expired on the rivet, not only were some competitors producing lesser-quality jeans with rivets, but they also perfectly replicated the Levi's® arcuate on the back pockets. This made it extremely hard for the increasingly discontented LS&Co. marketing team (who constantly tried to obtain updated market research) to distinguish their jeans from the mass of garments flooding the market. If it was hard for them to recognize a pair of LS&Co. jeans, imagine the minefield it must have been for consumers. Lucier's astute and ingenious idea was to place a piece of "folded cloth ribbon in the structural seam of a rear patch pocket."

This cloth was red in color, sewn into the right back pocket of the 501® jeans with the word "LEVI'S®" woven in white. There was no denying that the bold little red tab would stand out among the sea of indigo. This allowed the LS&Co. marketing team to produce more solid research while advertising to onlookers the wearers' brand choice. A range of in-store and outdoor advertising that displayed the message "Look for the Red Tab" was designed in the 1940s and 1950s. A message so strong that after more than seven decades, the iconic little red tab is as instantly recognizable as Lucier could ever have wished it would be—a crimson flag proudly displaying the excellent quality and craftsmanship of a garment that is now part of a global brand.

In 1967, Levi Strauss & Co. contracted Walter Landor & Associates to design a new housemark. The new batwing design mirrored the arcuate stitching on the back pocket of the jeans, and the word "LEVI'S®," which had always been in uppercase letters, was changed to "Levi's®." With only the "L" in uppercase, this now used the founder's name correctly. In turn, the red tab reflected this change. As denim heads will know, Levi jeans are labeled as "big E" or "little e" when dating a pair of Levi jeans. "Big E" refers to jeans made up until 1970–1971; "little e," jeans made after this period.

Out of all the elements of denim branding, the "Red Tab Device" is probably the most recognizable and most frequently copied. As such, in order to achieve maximum protection of the complete tab device, which encompasses the Levi's® wording and the company's exclusive legal right to market clothes with the tab, they have to produce a certain percentage of Levi's® products with just the ® symbol on a plain tab in order to maintain the trademark rights. However, there are some companies that pay a cheeky homage to the tab while staying within the legal confines. I had firsthand experience with this when I was putting on my first pair of Tellason jeans. The back pockets were facing up, and I noticed a small, faded, oblong outline that seemed to appear from the inside of the back pocket. I looked inside and was surprised to see a hidden red woven tab with the word "LeGAL" on it.

Post-1971 small "e" on selvage Lot 501 sample garment, 1980
Courtesy of Levi Strauss & Co. Archives.

One-side, red tab, men's waist overalls, Lot 501, 1947
Courtesy of Levi Strauss & Co. Archives

Orange tab on Lot 663 flares, 1972
Courtesy of Levi Strauss & Co. Archives

Silver tab, last season, spring 2011
Courtesy of Levi Strauss & Co. Archives

114

Reproduction woven labels used on Levi's® Vintage Clothing
Author's collection / Photographer Joey Seawell

Reproduction woven labels used on Levi's® Vintage Clothing
Author's collection / Photographer Joey Seawell

116

Lee® 91J jacket: This jacket was made between 1936 and 1939. The buttons were used as early as 1919 (or earlier). Several versions of this label were used, adding information such as "Jelt Denim" (1931) and "Sanforized Shrunk" (1936) as these terms were added to Lee® products and advertising.
Courtesy of Lee® Jeans / Photographer Bobbie Hamzioui

117

Lee® Jelt Denim, Sanforized: This jacket was made between 1940 and 1956.
Courtesy of Lee® Jeans / Photographer Bobbie Hamzioui

Lee® Union-Alls, 1960–1970
Courtesy of Lee® Jeans / Photographer Bobbie Hamzioui

Lee® Trademark Reg: These Whizit overalls were made between 1927 and 1935.
Courtesy of Lee® Jeans / Photographer Bobbie Hamzioui

Lee® Sanforized Shrunk: This pair of Cowboy Pants was made between 1938 and 1943. This cloth label was used on Lee® garments from 1936 to the late 1940s.
Courtesy of Lee® Jeans / Photographer Bobbie Hamzioui

Lee® 1960–1970: a capitalized "R" surrounded by a circle, called a "racol" for Registered & Authorized Company Logo, is the standard mark in the US to denote that a logo has been registered with the US Patent and Trademark Office. This mark cannot be used until after the government has issued a patent number or the mark has been registered or both. It is most widely seen in the Lee® collection (and has been used for dating here), especially in logos Lee® registered after the "tall E" logo, which was registered in 1960 (#709,990). This mark is used both on exterior and interior labels of garments and other materials produced by Lee®.
Courtesy of Lee® Jeans / Photographer Bobbie Hamzioui

Lee® Union-Alls (RMR), 1962–1972: The MR, or Marca Registrada, which appears after the "R" marking on product labels and elsewhere that the Lee® logo is used, is Spanish for trademark. It is believed that sometime after 1962, when Lee® started to sell garments in Mexico and Latin America, Lee® began to use labels with the "MR" in compliance with Mexican law (where the use of the MR is compulsory). However, the Lee® Westerner flashers, copyrighted in 1958, also show the RMR symbols.
Courtesy of Lee® Jeans / Photographer Bobbie Hamzioui

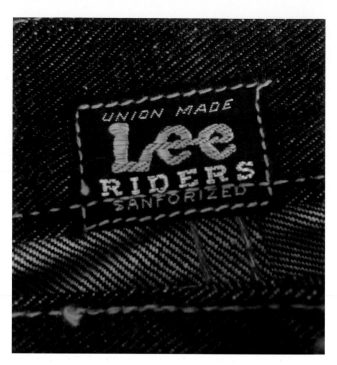

Lee® Guaranteed SHRUNK: Lee® woven product label in waistband
Courtesy of Lee® Jeans / Photographer Bobbie Hamzioui

Lee® Riders: Lee® 101 woven label in waistband, 1950–1969. Gold on black labels were introduced after 1950.
Courtesy of Lee® Jeans / Photographer Bobbie Hamzioui

Lee® Sanforized (gold and red on black): woven label on waistband, 1936–1940
Courtesy of Lee® Jeans / Photographer Bobbie Hamzioui

Lee® back pocket bartack (racol after Lee® on small label): This pair of jeans was made between 1950 and 1969. However, Lee® began using this style of bartack on back pockets in 1938. Lee®'s gold on black labels were introduced after 1950.
Courtesy of Lee® Jeans / Photographer Bobbie Hamzioui

Lee® 101LJ Storm Rider jacket label: This jacket was made between 1970 and 1980. Lee® first used the name Storm Rider for this jacket in 1954, though the design was introduced in 1952. Lee® rebranded the lined version of the 101J Cowboy Jacket, which featured an Alaskan blanket lining and a corduroy collar, starting in 1954, under the name Storm Rider. This name was protected under trademark law. The first use of the term "Storm Rider" was listed on the application to register the trademark for the term and logo design for outerwear jackets (men's, women's, boy's, girl's), filed with the US Patent & Trademark Office, which reports the first use as November 16, 1953. The trademark was registered February 22, 1955.
Courtesy of Lee® Jeans / Photographer Bobbie Hamzioui

Garment Workers Union label inside pocket, 1938
Courtesy of Lee® Jeans / Photographer Bobbie Hamzioui

Lee® pocket label: This jacket style was introduced in 1948. This example was made between 1970 and 1980. The Lee® label with racol has been used since 1960.
Courtesy of Lee® Jeans / Photographer Bobbie Hamzioui

Cant' Bust 'Em Gold Label on overalls, 1940–1949, likely made by Eloesser-Heynemann Company before Lee® bought E-H in 1946.
Courtesy of Lee® Jeans / Photographer Bobbie Hamzioui

Lee® RMR product label on Lee® overalls, 1962–1971. Lee® stopped using Sanforized on labels and price lists in 1972.
Courtesy of Lee® Jeans / Photographer Bobbie Hamzioui

1950s 888BJL woven size-and-brand
label for Blue Bell Wrangler (pre-1955)
Courtesy of Wrangler Archive /
Photographer Joey Seawell

1950s (pre-1955) overall iron-on chest label for Blue Bell
Courtesy of Wrangler Archive / Photographer Joey Seawell

1940s cyanic-blue screen, printed Blue Bell overalls chest label
Courtesy of Wrangler Archive / Photographer Joey Seawell

1950s (post-1955) men's western denim woven fly label
Courtesy of Wrangler Archive / Photographer Joey Seawell

1940s Rodeo Ben custom outfit made for the Appalachian Mountaineers, a bluegrass band from western North Carolina that toured and performed from the '30s through the '50s. In 1947, Blue Bell hired Rodeo Ben to be the designer of their yet-to-launch western brand, Wrangler, which would officially launch in 1949.
Courtesy of Wrangler Archive / Photographer Joey Seawell

8BJ woven Blue Bell Wrangler label (pre-1955)
Courtesy of Wrangler Archive / Photographer Joey Seawell

1950s iron-on Big Ben chest label
Courtesy of the Morrison Collection / Photographer Joey Seawell

1970s Lady Wrangler woven waistband, inset
label on embroidered jeans
Courtesy of Wrangler Archive / Photographer Joey Seawell

1930s J. C. Penney Co. Super Pay Day, 8 oz. woven chest label
Courtesy of the Morrison Collection / Photographer Joey Seawell

1950s 66MW Blue Bell Wrangler woven label inset into neck
Courtesy of Wrangler Archive / Photographer Joey Seawell

1950s 111MJ first edition men's western pleated-front jacket with actuating sleeves, produced by Blue Bell Wrangler, detail of Neolite Tag, hangar loop, and cloth model and lot label, LHT selvage 11 oz. denim
Courtesy of Wrangler Archive / Photographer Joey Seawell.

1940s Blue Bell girls Jeanies side-zip, denim waistband inset cloth size label detailing two-tone chain stitch yoke and 2x1 denim
Courtesy of Wrangler Archive / Photographer Joey Seawell

1970s Wrangler fly label (cloth) with size and wash instructions, 2x1 denim
Courtesy of Wrangler Archive / Photographer Joey Seawell

1950s Blue Bell coveralls in vat-dyed gray twill with gold chain stitching detail and cloth Blue Bell Sanforized neck label
Courtesy of Wrangler Archive / Photographer Joey Seawell

1950s 13MWZ Blue Bell Wrangler cloth woven label on fly, showing size, detailing fill yarn of 13 oz. LHT 3x1 denim
Courtesy of Wrangler Archive / Photographer Joey Seawell

Tellason Jeans pocket detail, worn, internal red tab showing on back pocket
Author's collection / Photographer Joey Seawell

Tellason Jeans pocket detail with internal red tab "LeGAL," a nod to the important heritage of Levi Strauss and Co.'s famous LEVIS/LeVIS red tab on jeans.
Author's collection / Photographer Joey Seawell

I noticed a small faded oblong outline that seemed to appear from the inside of the back pocket. I looked inside and was surprised to reveal a hidden red woven tab with the word "LeGAL."

–Nick Williams

Diesel product labels, c. 1990
Courtesy of Wouter Munnichs, founder of Long John *online magazine*

Eat Dust back neck woven label, c. 2017
Courtesy of Eat Dust / Photographer Thomas Skou

132

Woven label, c. 2017
Courtesy of Sam Poole, Iron Heart International Ltd.

Woven label, c. 2017
Courtesy of Sam Poole, Iron Heart International Ltd.

Dawson Denim woven label
Courtesy of Dawson Denim

Candiani Italian Premium Denim fabric identity label stitched
into one-piece fly construction, c. 2017
*Courtesy of Ali Kirby & Catharina Veder at
DENHAM the Jeanmaker*

Woven size label, c. 2017
Courtesy of Rogue Territory LLC

Sugar Cane & Co. back neck patch, 2016
Courtesy of photographer Shuhei Nomachi / TOYO Enterprise Co., Ltd.

WOVEN LABELS

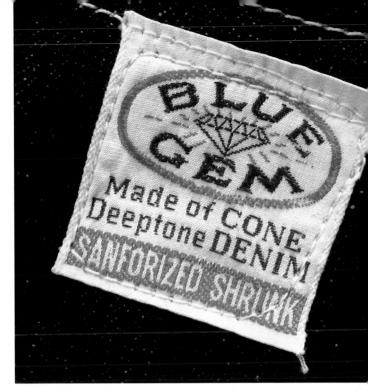

1940s co-branded Cone Deeptone Denim 8 oz. woven label
Courtesy of White Oak Archive Room—Cone Denim

Blue Gem overalls woven label
Courtesy of Cone Denim LLC, a division of International Textile Group

Evisu Heritage woven label: A nod to the iconic Lee® factory label
Courtesy of Evisu Group Limited

Stonewall overalls woven label
Courtesy of Cone Denim LLC, a division of International Textile Group

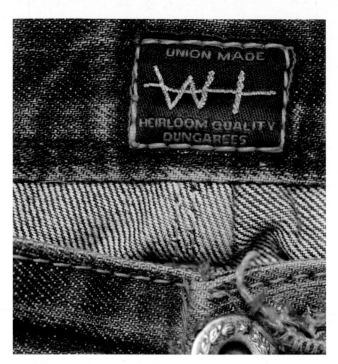

1930s Casey Jones Big 8 oz. Sanforized work dungaree made of Cone Deeptone Denims, detailing woven cloth Casey Jones waistband label
Courtesy of the Morrison Collection / Photographer Joey Seawell

2015 WH Ranch Dungarees 1936 Rodeo Ryder Jean, winner of Denim World Championship Artisan Challenge 2015–2017, detailing steel laurel wreath WWII donut button, WH Ranch woven label, and 3x1 shrink-to-fit Cone Denim
Courtesy of WH Ranch Dungarees Archives / Photographer Joey Seawell

Tellason Ladbroke waistband and fly with woven Tellason T Label and 3x1 denim
Author's collection / Photographer Joey Seawell

Deadstock Washington Dee Cee Sanforized 10 oz. denim overalls woven label, 1960s
Author's collection

136

BLKSMTH printed woven label at Loren Manufacturing Inc., Brooklyn, New York
Courtesy of Loren Cronk, photography by Martin Scott Powell

THE PATCH

Leather patches were standard during early jean production, right up until around the 1970s. Mass production hit and retail prices were driven down due to competitive selling, which resulted in less costly materials. Leather and hair-on-hide patches were replaced with Jacron (a paper material that looks like leather) and Neolite rubber versions.

Up until 1890, the leather patch on a pair of Levi Strauss & Co. jeans contained a description of the jeans as well as the company's name. The patent on the riveted blue jeans, owned by Jacob Davis and Levi Strauss & Co., expired in 1890. With this knowledge, LS&Co. needed to devise a way to cleverly convey to their customers the strength and high quality of their jeans before the market became flooded with competitors' versions. For some consumers, English was their second language, and in remote parts of the West, not everyone was literate, so the challenge was to communicate this message to everyone who wore blue jeans. The two-horse logo was created to clearly and instantly convey this. There was no doubting the outstanding quality of their jeans. The vivid image conjured up a catchy name for the jeans, and early consumers would walk into their general store requesting "those pants with the two horses." There was no other denim brand with such a symbol, and the consumers would always be handed over a pair of Levi's® jeans. That particular jean was called "the Two Horse® Brand" until 1928, at which time the company used its Levi's® trademark.

Among one of the many assets that adorned Lee® Jean's 101 Cowboy Pant in 1938 was their newly created hair-on-hide leather label. Not only did Lee® Jeans want to brand their name onto a leather patch, they created a way of leaving the hide on the leather and branding straight onto it. It took more than six months to perfect the branding method, but the result was a special piece of denim branding that is coveted by denim enthusiasts to this day.

Thankfully we are now seeing a resurgence in the use of thicker leather and hair-on-hide patches, as well as old techniques such as hot-iron branding by artisan and boutique denim brands, which elevate this piece of denim branding to a whole different aesthetic. There are also a lot of hidden (and not so hidden) meanings crafted into their work.

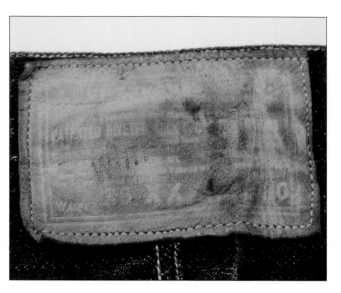

Leather patch design on denim waist overalls, January 1, 1879–December 31, 1879
Courtesy of Levi Strauss & Co. Archives

Two-horse trademark leather patch on deadstock, 1953 501XX
Courtesy of Levi Strauss & Co. Archives

Two-horse trademark on printed woven patch on Lot 201 men's waist overalls, January 1901–December 1921
Courtesy of Levi Strauss & Co. Archives

Boss of the Road waistband patch, 1920–1939. Eloesser-Henemann registered the trademark for this Boss of the Road patch design in 1919.
Courtesy of Lee® Jeans / Photographer Bobbie Hamzioui

140

Twitch Leather Label

The cut and construction of the 101 pant changed very little after 1941, though its name and some of Lee's signature details did. In 1944, Lee advertisements reflect a change in the way it calls out the hair-on-hide label, last seen in January 1944 on the back right waistband, to a smooth leather label, calling it the "Hot Iron Branded Cowhide Label" (April 1944). Instead of a patch with the hair still on the hide, the new patch was smooth, and the leather was branded with a wavy Lee logo. The new "brand" was made with the three letters connected, from the "L" across the lowercase "e"s. The H. D. Lee Company files an application with the US Patent office to trademark the "twitch" logo on November 7, 1945. The application states that it was first used on November 2, 1945. The trademark was registered June 24, 1947, and continued to be used at least through the year 2000.

–Jean Svadlenak, consultant to museums, Lee® Jeans

Lee® product label hair-on-hide waistband patch: Lee® 101 waistband overalls featuring hair-on-hide labels were made between 1938 and 1945.
Courtesy of Lee® Jeans / Photographer Bobbie Hamzioui

Lee® product label, Lee® Twitch waistband patch: This pair of jeans was made between 1950 and 1969. The hot-iron-branded leather Twitch label was introduced in 1945, when H. D. Lee® Company filed an application with the US Patent and Trademark office for trademark. The application was filed on November 7, 1945, and states that the logo was first used on November 2, 1945. Continues in use.
Courtesy of Lee® Jeans / Photographer Bobbie Hamzioui

141

Lee® product label Red Ribbon leather waistband patch: This patch was used from 1925 to 1938, and this particular pair of Lee® 101 waistband Cowboy Overalls was made in 1938.
Courtesy of Lee® Jeans / Photographer Bobbie Hamzioui

Lee® Product Label, Lee® 131 Cowboy Overalls waistband patch: Lee® made 131 cowboy waistband overalls from 1931 to 1944.
Courtesy of Lee® Jeans / Photographer Bobbie Hamzioui

Lee® Riders Cowboy Pants "Burn Your Own Brand," 1946
Courtesy of Lee® Jeans / Photographer Bobbie Hamzioui

Lee® Riders: Lee® offered these pants from 1938 to 1959. This pair is from 1946. An added feature on the new hair-on-hide Cowboy Pants for boys was a second leather patch where you could "burn your own brand." The Fall & Winter 1938–39 Ario's Cowboy Catalog #43 (above) advertised a leather label on the back left pocket of boys' Cowboy Pants that can be branded with "your brand or initials or both, free of charge." Special instructions came with each pair. Lee® targeted Boy Scouts with some ads, stating, "burn your troop number on your favorite pair of jeans.

–Jean Svadlenak, courtesy of Lee® Jeans

111MJ Blue Bell Wrangler pleated western jacket in new old stock with neolite Blue Bell Wrangler label sewn and cloth lot and size label inset into collar
Courtesy of Wrangler Archive / Photographer Joey Seawell

144

1950s Blue Bell Wrangler MWZ pocket flasher artwork with neolite patch, denoting 14 oz. denim
Courtesy of Wrangler Archive / Photographer Joey Seawell

1950s 22MWZ in light-blue denim, Blue Bell Wrangler western jeans with neolite label, "W" stitch, extra reinforcement for pocket strength, and nickel-finished scratch-proof rivets
Courtesy of Wrangler Archive / Photographer Joey Seawell

1970s Lady Wrangler neolite pocket label
Courtesy of Wrangler Archive / Photographer Joey Seawell

1950s 11MJ neolite Blue Bell Wrangler label on acid-washed jacket
Courtesy of Wrangler Archive / Photographer Joey Seawell

Diesel Old Glory product label, c. 1990
Courtesy of Wouter Munnichs, founder of Long John *online magazine*

DENHAM the Jeanmaker chrome-free, soft-tempered Napa cow leather made in Italy, c. 2017
Courtesy of Ali Kirby & Catharina Veder at DENHAM the Jeanmaker

DENHAM the Jeanmaker Italian pure white leather patch overpainted in indigo ink, brushed back to white, leaving ink residue in the debossed logo, c. 2017.
Courtesy of Ali Kirby & Catharina Veder at DENHAM the Jeanmaker

Sugar Cane & Co. leather waistband patch,
c. 2016
*Courtesy of photographer Shuhei Nomachi /
TOYO Enterprise Co., Ltd.*

Sugar Cane & Co. leather waistband patch,
c. 2016
*Courtesy of photographer Shuhei Nomachi /
TOYO Enterprise Co., Ltd.*

Sugar Cane & Co. hair-on-hide waistband patch, c. 2016
*Courtesy of photographer Shuhei Nomachi /
TOYO Enterprise Co., Ltd.*

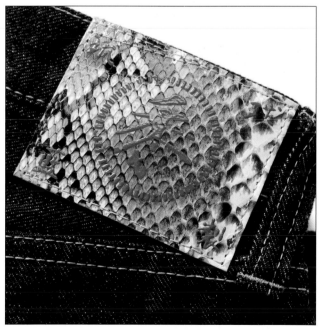

Sugar Cane & Co. snakeskin waistband patch, c. 2016
*Courtesy of photographer Shuhei Nomachi /
TOYO Enterprise Co., Ltd.*

Eat Dust hair-on-hide waistband patch, c. 2017
Courtesy of Eat Dust / Photographer Thomas Skou

Eat Dust women's leather patch, c. 2017
Courtesy of Eat Dust / Photographer Thomas Skou

Kings of Indigo leather patch, c. 2017
Courtesy of Kings of Indigo

Kings of Indigo leather patch, c. 2017
Courtesy of Kings of Indigo

Denim World Championship-winning pair for Artisan Challenge by W.H. Ranch Dungarees: This pair features 12 oz. Cone XX shrink-to-fit denim, original pattern for 1933 Lee® cowboy jeans with arcuate stitch, blank label for ranch branding (branded "DWC"), cinch buckle back, triple stiched, with X tacks for pocket reinforcement.
Courtesy of W.H. Ranch Dungarees Archive / Photographer Joey Seawell

THE PATCH

Denim World Championship-winning pair
Courtesy of W.H. Ranch Dungarees Archive / Photographer Joey Seawell

2010s Tellason Ladbroke Grove slim-tapered jeans, showing leather patch from Portland-based Tanner Goods and designed by Brian Awitan with Andy Cruz at House Industries, using type face Benguiat Buffalo. Inset paper label for lot and cloth type, denoting lot 101.03 and cloth 14.75 oz Cone White Oak denim. The jean's style name, Ladbroke Grove, comes from Tony Patella and Pete Searson's love for the Clash. Ladbroke Grove is the neighborhood where members of the band lived when they formed. Lot number 101 for the 101'ers (the band Joe Strummer was in before the Clash). The Tellason name is a mash-up of Tony and Pete's last names.

Author's collection / Photographer Joey Seawell

154

Rogue Territory feather logo on leather patch, c. 2016
Courtesy of Rogue Territory LLC

The Feather Logo

Just like the lasso stitch and the pen pocket, the feather wasn't established until I started thinking about a jean that I wanted to see on the shelves in denim stores. When I was young, my parents hung these four prints in the room I shared with my brother. They depicted cowboys rounding up cattle, a rider on a bucking bronco, and a Native American wearing a headdress and holding a bow and arrow. I fell in love with these images from the moment I set eyes on them, and consequently this started my love affair with the Wild West and the stories of Lone Ranger and all the infamous outlaws. When I opened the Rogue Territory Work Shop in American Rag, my parents sent me these prints to hang on the walls. Though I love the entire series, the Native American was always the one that I loved the most. So I wanted to figure out a way to incorporate what I love about the image into a logo for Rogue Territory. I wasn't about to use his likeness or offend anybody by using the headdress, so I essentially plucked a feather out of the head dress and that became my logo and the tie to this piece of art.

–Karl Thoennessen, Rogue Territory LLC

Dawson Denim leather patch, c. 2016
Courtesy of Dawson Denim

The branding was always to be a combination of our love of vintage motoring and denim; the logo is from the lever off a turn-of-the-century motorcycle called the Bat, designed by Bat Motor Manufacturing Co. Ltd. (1902). It's a cheesehead screw that was holding the lever to the motorcycle; we liked what it symbolized. The rest was inspired by Kelly's 1957 BSA Bantam.

–Scott Ogden & Kelly Dawson, Dawson Denim

156

Endrime leather patch
Courtesy of Endrime

Not many denim brands use real leather on their back patch—let alone hand brand their own patch in-house with a hot branding iron. This is something we wanted to revert back to when establishing Endrime. The Kufic "MOHSIN SAJID" circle stamp was designed and developed in early 2011. Many versions of the Kufic logo were created; the more traditional square type was considered, but it was decided early on to do a more untraditional circle Kufic logo instead. Its designed in a circle so it becomes infinite—an early mystical concept that Muslims believe leads back to God, as God is infinite.

–Mohsin Sajid, Endrime

Endrime hand-branded leather patch with hot branding iron
Courtesy of Endrime

Left Field coal miner printed leather patch
Courtesy of Christian McCann, Left Field NYC

[There is a] miner theme throughout the denim. I grew up a couple hours from Coal Country, PA [Pennsylvania], in Philly. When I was doing the denim collection I wanted to represent workwear from an East Coast perspective. Levi's® and all the throwback West Coast repro brands generally portray denim with a romantic gold miner or cowboy theme, and I wanted something down and dirty to reflect the Philly side of me. Coal mining was close by, and there's nothing romantic about coal mining, but it does represent some of the most badass American workers in our history, and I wanted to bring the struggle and story to the surface, which is generally overlooked in that field of mining. Some of the best, cleanest, hardest, and longest-burning coal was found a few hours from Philly and is called anthracite. During the turn of the century it was the mecca for coal mining. Many Irish immigrants came over to the US and took jobs working in the Pennsylvania coal mines, working for pennies a day in almost complete darkness in damp and extremely dangerous environments; succumbing to death in methane explosions, roof collapses, or accidents; or suffering an early death from black lung and the inability to get air in their lungs. I bring in pictures and stories through social media and other avenues about the hardship of the miners and the miserable existence they lived. Families lived in rundown coal patch shacks owned by the company, and were paid in coal script (company money that could be used only in the company store). God forbid they were killed in an accident; the mine would bring them home dead in a Black Maria (a black, horse-drawn wagon), where they would throw the dead miner's body on the front porch and settle the debt the following week, which usually consisted of eviction and sometimes becoming indentured servants to the mines until their debts were paid off. Black Maria is also what we call our black sulfur warp-and-weft selvage denim, using all black hardware and a black-leather miner label. We have an original Pennsylvania coal cart in our shop, including anthracite coal, antique picks, oil lamps, candle holders, detonators, lunch pails, a child's leather mining hat, coal script, coal tags (identifying who mined the coal in the carts), wood boxes that held dynamite, and many other antique miner collectibles.

–Christian McCann, Left Field NYC

Butcher hook logo cloth patch
Courtesy of Butcher of Blue

Evisu cloth patch, date unknown
Courtesy of Evisu Group Limited

The One Jeans patch with traditional hot branding iron, c. 2014
Courtesy of Mark Westmoreland The One Goods/ Photograph by Ben Monk

Iron Heart leather patch, c. 2017
Courtesy of Sam Poole, Iron Heart International Ltd.

Leather patch at Loren Manufacturing Inc., Brooklyn, New York
Courtesy of Loren Cronk, photography by Martin Scott Powell

BLKSMTH leather label at Loren Manufacturing Inc., Brooklyn, New York
Courtesy of Loren Cronk photography by Martin Scott Powell

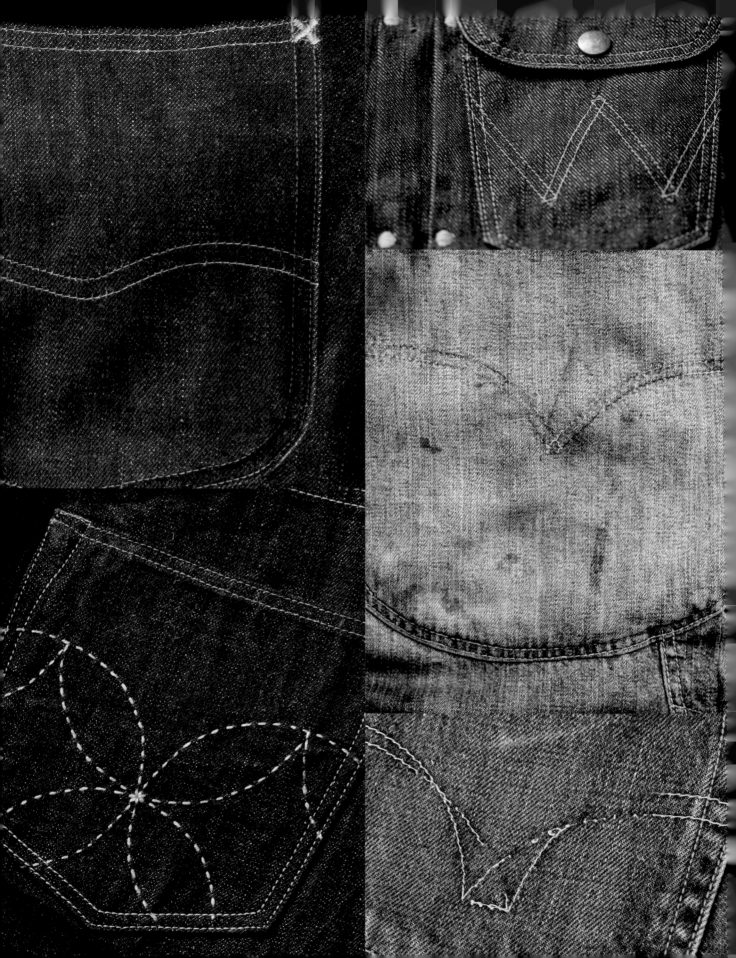

THE ARCUATE

The arcuate is another type of branding and design associated with jeanswear. Even without any other means of identifying a pair of jeans, the arcuate stitching is a clear branding statement. It is possible that Levi Strauss & Co. was the very first denim brand to use the arcuate. The earliest pair of waist overalls within the Levi Strauss & Co. archive that includes an arcuate dates from 1879. Due to the 1906 earthquake and fire in San Francisco, many of the company's documents were destroyed. It is not certain why the arcuate was designed for the back pocket, but it is possible that it was created as part of the reinforcement and possibly to secure the pocket lining. Equally unknown is why the arcuate was designed as such.

The arcuate would have originally been sewn on by sewing-machine workers and then later by double-needle machines in the mid-1950s, which produced the "diamond" stitch effect.

Early denim brands replicated this same design, again, seeing it as a denim-branding standard until Levi Strauss & Co. trademarked the design in 1943 and all other brands were forced to stop using it. In 1944, Lee® introduced their own unique back pocket stitching, named the Lazy "S," which resembled the shape of the horns of a longhorn. Blue Bell Wrangler's early prototype-era jeans (1947–1949) carried the Levi's®-style arcuate until they formally launched Wrangler in 1949, at which time they began stitching two Ws, one on each back pocket, which represents Western Wear.

During World War II, the US government deemed the arcuate as decorative and nonfunctional. To conserve the thread, the arcuate was removed during wartime. Levi Strauss & Co. maintained the design by having the sewing-machine workers paint the arcuate onto the back pockets.

Modern denim brands continue the tradition of designing their versions of the arcuate.

Arcuate stitch design on Nevada waist overalls back pocket, 1880s
Courtesy of Levi Strauss & Co. Archives

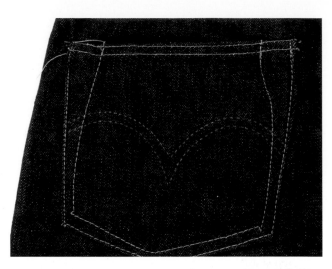

Painted arcuate design during World War II on Lot 501® men's waist overall, 1944
Courtesy of Levi Strauss & Co. Archives

Lee® Cowboy Overalls back-pocket stitching: This pair of Lee® 101 waistband Cowboy Overalls was made in 1938. "X"-stitched tacks replaced metal rivets on the back pockets in 1938 to prevent scratches on furniture and saddles. Stitching on back pockets was not standardized until the 1940s. This pocket stitching is much less pronounced than the original arcuate design used by Lee® and others, and suggests the early beginnings of the Lazy "S" Lee® became famous for. The orange thread was used on Lee® Cowboy Overalls in the 1920s through the late 1930s.
Courtesy of Lee® Jeans / Photographer Bobbie Hamzioui

Lee® back-pocket stitching: Lee® 131 Cowboy Overalls, 1931–1940. This pair was made in 1938—bartack rivets on pockets. This straight-line back-pocket stitch pattern was common on Lee® work wear (overalls, Union-Alls).
Courtesy of Lee® Jeans / Photographer Bobbie Hamzioui

Lazy S Compound Curve

In 1943—at the height of World War II, Levi Strauss & Co. trademarked the arcuate stitch on back pockets, forcing Lee and other manufacturers of cowboy pants to establish their own signature stitch for back pockets. For a time, Lee flipped the arcuate-style top-stitching on back pockets briefly, which likely was challenged by Levi Strauss & Co. Material shortages—threads, fabrics, and metals—during the war also caused manufacturers to cut back on decorative use of thread and other materials, and for a period, Lee's back pockets had no decorative stitching, though it is difficult to determine precisely when or for how long. (Paper shortages meant that Lee didn't print price lists as frequently, and salesmen relied on annually typed price lists for information—making research challenging in verifying exactly when changes occurred during World War II.) Print ads show some changes between mid-1945 and April 1946. Beginning in April 1946, Lee rebranded cowboy pants as Lee Riders and likely introduced both the Twitch (trademarked in 1946, starting first use November 1945) and added the Lazy S compound-curve back pocket at the same time. When the stitches on both back pockets are viewed together, they resemble the shape of longhorn cattle horns. Images of the back pockets in print ads are clues to when these changes occurred.

–Jean Svadlenak, consultant to museums, Lee Jeans

Lee® back-pocket stitching: Lee®'s Lazy "S" pocket stitching was introduced in 1944. This pair: 1946–1955.
Courtesy of Lee® Jeans / Photographer Bobbie Hamzioui

Lee® 101 button-fly Cowboy Pants/Jeans, with Lee®'s Lazy "S" pocket stitching. This pair: 1950–1969.
Courtesy of Lee® Jeans / Photographer Bobbie Hamzioui

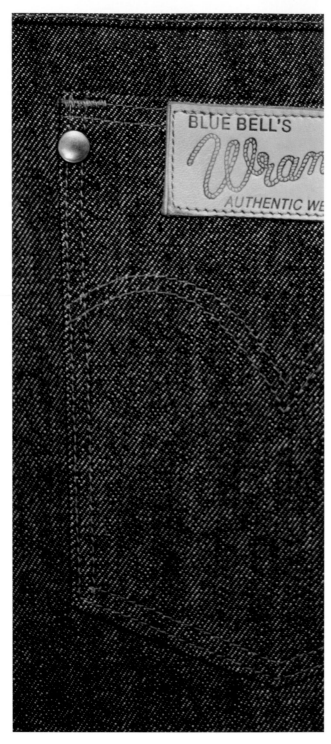

11MW prototype by Blue Bell Wrangler: Note the possessive of "Blue Bell," the bartack, and the domed, scratch-proof rivet, as well as the arcuate stitch.
Courtesy of the Morrison Collection / Photographer Joey Seawell

1940s prototype-era 11MW with steel rivet with copper finish
Courtesy of Wrangler Archive / Photographer Joey Seawell

Clockwise from top left:
1950s (pre-1955) 111MJ pocket with W stitch and Scovill Fasteners Gripper® Snap Fastener in copper finish with Wrangler roped logo; 1950s (post-1955) second-edition 27MW slant pocket with W stitch and Scovill Fasteners Gripper® Snap Fastener in white-enamel-painted finish over nickel; 1950s (post-1955) 66MW with W stitch and diamond-shaped Scovill Fasteners Gripper® Snap Fastener pearl snap in nickel finish; and 1950s (pre-1955) 11MJ pocket with W stitch and Scovill Fasteners Gripper® Snap Fastener in copper finish with Wrangler roped logo.
Courtesy of Wrangler Archive / Photographer Joey Seawell

Rogue Territory Lasso stitch, c. 2008
Courtesy of Rogue Territory LLC

The Origins of the Lasso Stitch

While I was sewing my first pair of jeans, apprenticing under my teacher "mentor" Brian Kim, I wanted to include all the denim head details. At this time, it was all about selvage and hidden rivets. These are the details I fell in love with. So, not knowing much about denim construction or how to apply rivets to the back panels of the jeans and then "hide" them with the back pocket, I just went for it. I applied the rivets and proceeded to sew down the pocket. The first pass (outside stitch) was a success! Then I started sewing the second stitch, and as I got closer to the hem and where the rivet was, I realized I was too close to the burr, so instead of ripping out the stitch and starting again I started to sew away from the edge of the pocket and the rivet in a curve, and after about 5/8" I needed to go back, so I wound up making a little loop and heading back up to the hem on the pocket. That's when the Lasso was born. It took about three years to get it to where it is today, tweaking, refining, and modifying, but that's where it came from. I didn't really use it that much until I started thinking about what I wanted my jeans to look like when I decided to create a ready-made collection.

–Karl Thoennessen, Rogue Territory LLC

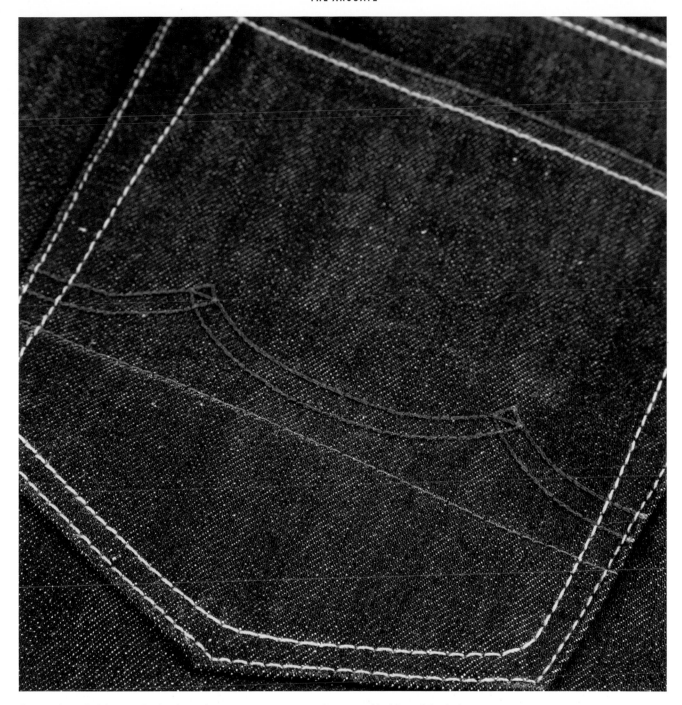

Decorative stitching on the back pockets represents water, the natural habitat of the koi carp.
Courtesy of Kings of Indigo

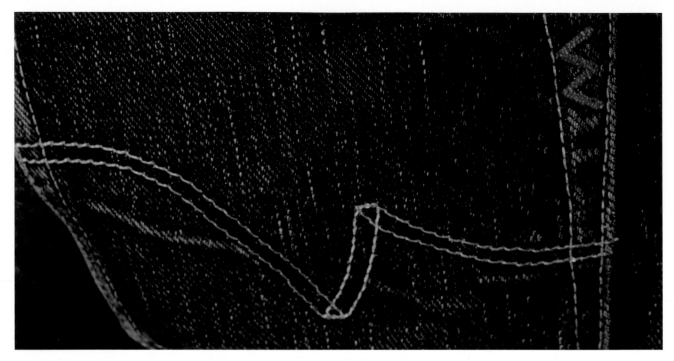

Iron Heart pocket stitching
Courtesy of Sam Poole, Iron Heart International Ltd.

Diesel Old Glory pocket stitching, c. 1990
Courtesy of Wouter Munnichs, founder of Long John *online magazine*

Motorcycle-inspired pocket stitching
Courtesy of Eat Dust / Photographer Thomas Skou

Sugar Cane & Co. Shippo pattern, Seven Treasure pocket stitching by hand, 2016
Courtesy of photographer Shuhei Nomachi / TOYO Enterprise Co., Ltd.

A butcher's hook inside the back pocket is revealed as the denim fades, c. 2012.
Courtesy Butcher of Blue

Evisu was founded in Osaka, Japan, in 1991 and is named after the Japanese god of prosperity, Ebisu. Initially only around fourteen pairs of jeans were created a day, each one caringly hand-painted with the now-famous seagull logo.
Courtesy of Evisu Group Limited

1950s Blue Bell Wrangler prototype boys' three-pocket, blanket-lined jacket, detailing blank copper buttons, straight-line pocket stitching, and welt pocket
Courtesy of Wrangler Archive / Photographer Joey Seawell

1950s Blue Bell Wrangler 27BW western shirt with enamel-painted W Grippet Snap buttons.
Courtesy of the Morrison Collection / Photographer Joey Seawell

Opposite page:
1930s Casey Jones Big 8 oz. Sanforized Cone Deeptone Denim work dungaree, detailing UFO rivets, arcuate stitch, buckle back cinch closure, and 2x1 denim
Courtesy of the Morrison Collection / Photographer Joey Seawell

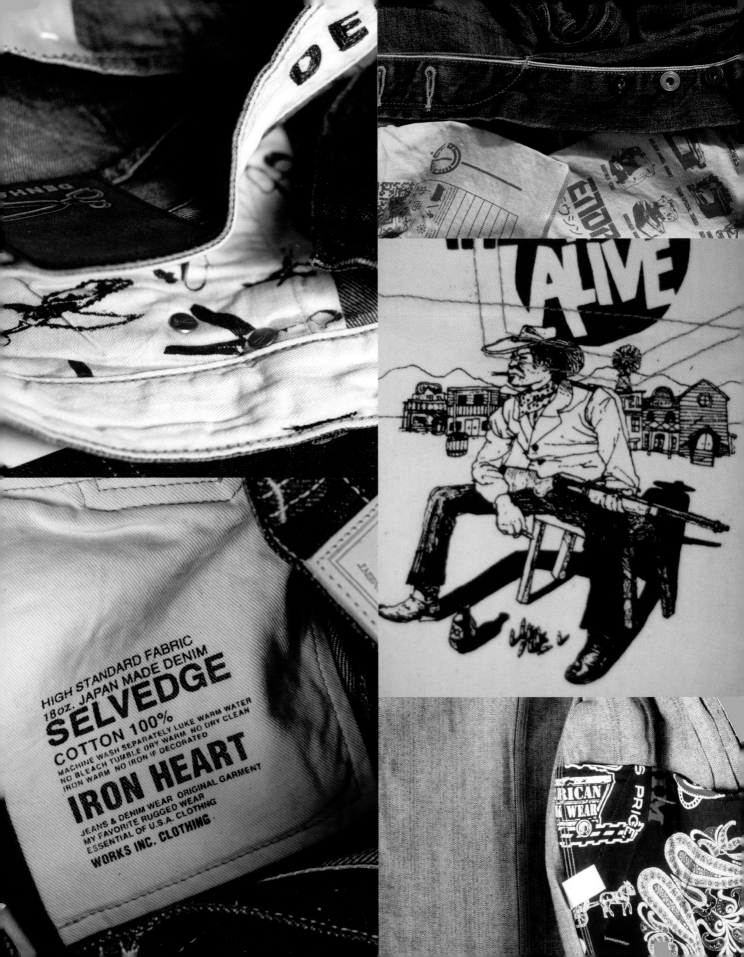

PRINTING

Some of the information and graphics printed on the original Levi Strauss & Co.'s guarantee ticket was extracted from the inside pocket bag of their waist overalls. Prior to 1892, the pocket bag was the only denim-branding element that contained the image of the Two Horse® logo, information about the fabric and fit, and other elements. It was a way for LS&Co. to inform the customer about the high quality of their waist overalls and for them to stand out among the competition.

Today, the pocket bag is no less informative; in fact, this early form of denim branding is being used by some brands as a canvas to tell their story and to connect with their customers. Some current brands have the traditional informative content about the makeup of the jean printed on the pocket bag; others have their logo or a specially commissioned piece of artwork. There are some boutique brands that use this part of the jean to explain exactly how the jean was constructed or how and why the brand was created. Endrime, whose main brand ethos is transparency, prints onto the pocket bag every machine that was used in the production of that jean, as well as a wash story on the opposite side.

Printing isn't exclusive to the pocket bag; Left Field's beautiful bandana design is printed on the exterior of the side pockets and Evisu famously prints on the inside back of some of their jeans.

Printing on denim is another piece of branding that adds to the romance of the maker. A lot of printing placed directly onto denim is hidden; it is waiting to be discovered. Whether it is a hidden rivet, a flash of colored enamel on the back of a button, or a pocket bag print, all these details add interest and value to the wearer and show them how much they care about their brand and how much thought has gone into the creation and design of the article.

Scissor-art-printed fishbone pocketing and yoke panel
Courtesy of Ali Kirby & Catharina Veder at
DENHAM the Jeanmaker

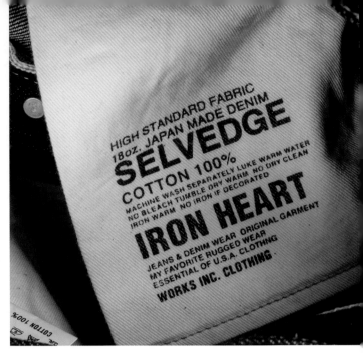

Pocket bag print
Courtesy of Sam Poole, Iron Heart International Ltd.

Pocket bag print
Courtesy of Eat Dust / Photographer Thomas Skou

Pocket bag print
Courtesy of Sam Poole, Iron Heart International Ltd.

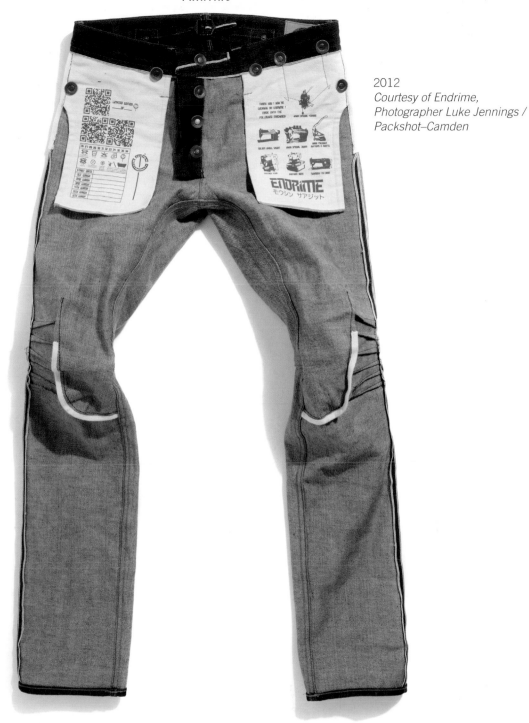

2012
*Courtesy of Endrime,
Photographer Luke Jennings /
Packshot–Camden*

One of Endrime's main brands ethos is transparency—and all garments are made with special attention to the inside. One of the key features is that all the machines that are used in production are listed/stamped inside the pants pocket bag. Something no other brand does. The wash story is stamped on the opposite side.

–Mohsin Sajid, Endrime

179

Pocket bag print on Denim World Championship-winning pair for Artisan Challenge by W.H. Ranch Dungarees, using 12 oz. Cone XX shrink-to-fit denim, original pattern for 1933 Lee® cowboy jeans, with arcuate stitch, hair-on-hide label branded "WH," cinch buckle back, triple stitched, with X tacks for pocket reinforcement.
Courtesy of W.H. Ranch Dungarees Archive / Photographer Joey Seawell

180

 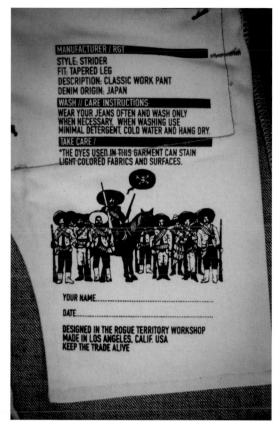

Printed pocket bag
Courtesy of Rogue Territory LLC

Through collaborations and exclusive releases with friends and artists, we strive to bring awareness to those who take pride in perfecting their trade. "Keep the Trade Alive" is our way of featuring talented craftsmen and women who inspire us through their passion and dedication to their creative fields.

For some time now we've wanted to incorporate our love for spaghetti westerns, the Old West, and gunslingers into the product we produce.

We reached out to past collaborator William Goldwin to help us translate the idea of "Keep the Trade Alive" into a piece of artwork inspired in large part by The Man with No Name *trilogy starring Clint Eastwood. The final presentation was a true collaborative effort that features William's strong point of view as an artist and tells a story that we've wanted to convey through a medium that is underutilized in the denim industry—the blank canvas that is the inside of your jeans.*

–Karl Thoennessen, Rogue Territory LLC

Evisu famously prints on the inside back of some of their jeans.
Courtesy of Evisu Group Limited

Printed artwork on Diesel product, date unknown
Courtesy of Wouter Munnichs, founder of Long John *online magazine*

Left Field custom coal miner bandanna-printed pocket lining, c. 2016
Courtesy of Christian McCann, Left Field NYC

ZIP PULL

There are two major companies that supplied hardware to the founding denim brands that are still in existence today, Scovill Fasteners (whom we have already mentioned) and Talon. Established in Chicago in 1893, Talon was originally known as the Universal Fastener Company. They produced hookless fasteners for boots and shoes. The company moved to Meadville, Pennsylvania, and it is here that the zipper as we know it was invented, thanks to Swedish engineer Gideon Sunback. He was hired to improve the efficiency of the machines that were used to manufacture the fasteners, and ended up completely redesigning the product itself into something that is essentially the same as the modern metal-toothed zipper. The company was reorganized and chartered under the name the Hookless Fastener Company in 1913. They later adopted the Talon brand for their line of metal zippers in 1928, and the name of the company itself was changed to Talon Incorporated in 1938.

Talon supplied major denim brands such as Levi Strauss & Co., Carhartt, and Sweet Orr, but it was the H. D. Lee® Mercantile Company that made a major impact in the denim community when it partnered with Hookless Fastener Company. H. D. Lee® Mercantile is credited for being the first denim brand to incorporate a zip fly into a pair of waist overalls in 1927. We can deduce that the zipper was supplied by the Hookless Fastener Company from magazine ads for the waist overalls dated 1927, which feature drawings of the zipper sliders that clearly show the "HOOKLESS" logo on the pull. As previously mentioned, at this time Talon was still known as the Hookless Fastener Company.

Featuring a brand logo on the zip pull is just one of the many creative ways to incorporate denim branding. Lucky Brand Jeans have their shamrock logo cut into the zip pull, as well as a fabric label sewn into the inside of the zip fly with the words "Lucky You." Puma and Evisu's jean collaboration featured a Puma logo and an Evisu logo-shaped zip pull.

Not only are zips a functional addition to a pair of jeans, but they allow the designers to add their own personal touch and detail that, when part of the consideration of branding a pair of jeans, results in immense value for the wearer.

Lee® 101 zipper-fly Cowboy Pants/Jeans, 1950–1969: The first reference to a zipper fly style was 101-Z, which appeared in October 1949. The following year, Price List #64 was the first printed price list with the zipper fly style referred to as 101-Z. Button fly was still simply 101, and 101B was still used only for boys' sizes.
Courtesy of Lee® Jeans / Photographer Bobbie Hamzioui

Talon zip puller for Lee® jeans
Courtesy of Talon

The Hookless Fastener zip puller
Courtesy of Talon

In 1889, Henry David Lee®, along with four business partners, established the H. D. Lee® Mercantile Company, a grocery wholesale business, in Salina, Kansas. They quickly added sewing notions, fabric, furnishings, stationary, and school supplies to their inventory. Frustrated by unpredictable delivery from workwear suppliers, Lee® opened a factory in 1912 to produce jackets and work trousers (often called waist overalls at that time). Lee®'s sales grew exponentially after they introduced the first one-piece coverall, the Lee® "Union-All," in 1913. With the success of the Union-All, *Lee® expanded its workwear line of products.*

In 1924, the H. D. Lee® Mercantile Company designed its iconic 101 Cowboy Waist Overall to serve the American cowboy—a growing market in the American West. The 101 Cowboy Waist Overalls, a 9 oz. denim, copper-riveted pant, first appeared in Lee® salesmen's Price Lists in September 1925. Like cowboy pants by other manufacturers, the Lee® 101 had a button-fly front. In 1927, Lee® introduced Cowboy Pants, Union-Alls, and Overalls with a zip-front—the first in the United States—for men and boys. The New "Whizit Cowboy Waistband Overalls" was originally listed in the 1927 Price List as the Lee® 1010 Cowboy Pant, and Lee® offered both zip- and button-fly styles. At the same time, Lee® started offering their Cowboy Pants with inseam measurements for a more personal fit. By 1929, Lee® dropped the extra "0" and they became known simply as the Lee® 101. The Lee® 101 pant was redesigned to a more fitted style in 1941, becoming the 101 Lee® Rider—a name Lee® began using in 1935— though the name "Rider" didn't appear in Lee® advertising until after World War II, when a major marketing campaign was launched in 1946. Many denim lovers refer to all Lee® zip-fly pants as the 101Z. Lee® first used "101-Z" for its zip-fly style in its October 1949 price list.

–Jean Svadlenak, museum consultant, and Lee® Jeans archivist & historian

Lee® Union-Alls zipper pull, 1960–1970
Courtesy of Lee® Jeans /
Photographer Bobbie Hamzioui

Lee® Union-Alls zipper pull: This jacket was made between 1940 and 1956. *Courtesy of Lee® Jeans / Photographer Bobbie Hamzioui*

1970s/80s Talon 42 mark brass
Courtesy of Wrangler Archive / Photographer Joey Seawell

ZIP PULL

1950s Prentice brass zipper
Courtesy of Wrangler Archive / Photographer Joey Seawell

1960s/70s Scovill Fasteners zipper in nickel/zinc
Courtesy of Wrangler Archive / Photographer Joey Seawell

1950s Scovill Fasteners Gripper Zipper in brass
Courtesy of Wrangler Archive / Photographer Joey Seawell

Evisu logo zip pull from Puma and Evisu's collaboration,
c. 2006. *Courtesy of Mark Westmoreland*

189

SELVAGE

Lee® 101 Cowboy Pants/Jeans selvage edge seams, 1949–1959
Courtesy of Lee® Jeans / Photographer Bobbie Hamzioui

As part of the journey in creating this book, we traveled to Greensboro, North Carolina, to visit not only Wrangler but also the Cone Mills' White Oak Plant. The original mill that supplied Levi Strauss & Co. their denim fabric (including the famous high-quality XX fabric that was used on the very first pair of XX 501 in 1890) was Amoskeag Manufacturing Company of Manchester, New Hampshire. Cone Mills took over as their main supplier in 1915. It was an honor to be invited to tour America's oldest-running denim mill. My favorite part of the tour, as I am sure it is for many, was witnessing the hallowed shuttle looms busily at work, as they always had been for more than one hundred years. The rhythmic beat and vibration of the antique draper looms working in earnest to produce the selvage fabric was hypnotic. That, combined with the old wooden floor on which they stood, resulted in a unique selvage fabric that is currently impossible to perfectly replicate with modern machinery.

It is common knowledge that around 1927, Cone Mills had red yarn woven into the self-finishing edge (selvage) of the "extra durable" XX-fabric to easily identify it among the various bolts of fabric that they produced. As a result it became synonymous with Levi Strauss & Co., further affirming the brand's long-lasting quality.

Cone then started to use different-colored yarns to denote the varying shades, weights, and width of denim that they produced. In more-recent years, some denim brands and fashion houses have personalized the selvage on their jeans with their own unique colored yarn (or yarns) as a further branding technique.

At the time of writing this book, it was sadly announced that the White Oak Plant would cease operations at the end of 2017.

MADE IN U S A

CONE
deeptone*
DENIM

•SANFORIZED•

RESIDUAL SHRINKAGE NOT MORE THAN 1%

A

CONE*
FABRIC

•®CONE MILLS INC NEW YORK, N Y

28/29″ No. 27

10 oz. per sq. yd.

Eat Dust selvage ID
Courtesy of Eat Dust / Photographer Thomas Skou

Selvage busted outseam shot of Tellason unworn jeans
Author's collection / Photographer Joey Seawell

Selvage ID
Courtesy of Christian McCann, Left Field NYC

SELVAGE

Lee® 101 Waistband Overalls selvage edge seams, 1938–1945
Courtesy of Lee® Jeans / Photographer Bobbie Hamzioui

Sugar Cane & Co. selvage, 2016
Courtesy of photographer Shuhei Nomachi / TOYO Enterprise Co., Ltd.

Selvage ID lines
Courtesy of Evisu Group Limited

Opposite page:
Selvage denim rolls at Loren Manufacturing Inc., Brooklyn, NY
Courtesy of Loren Cronk, photography by Martin Scott Powell

SELVAGE

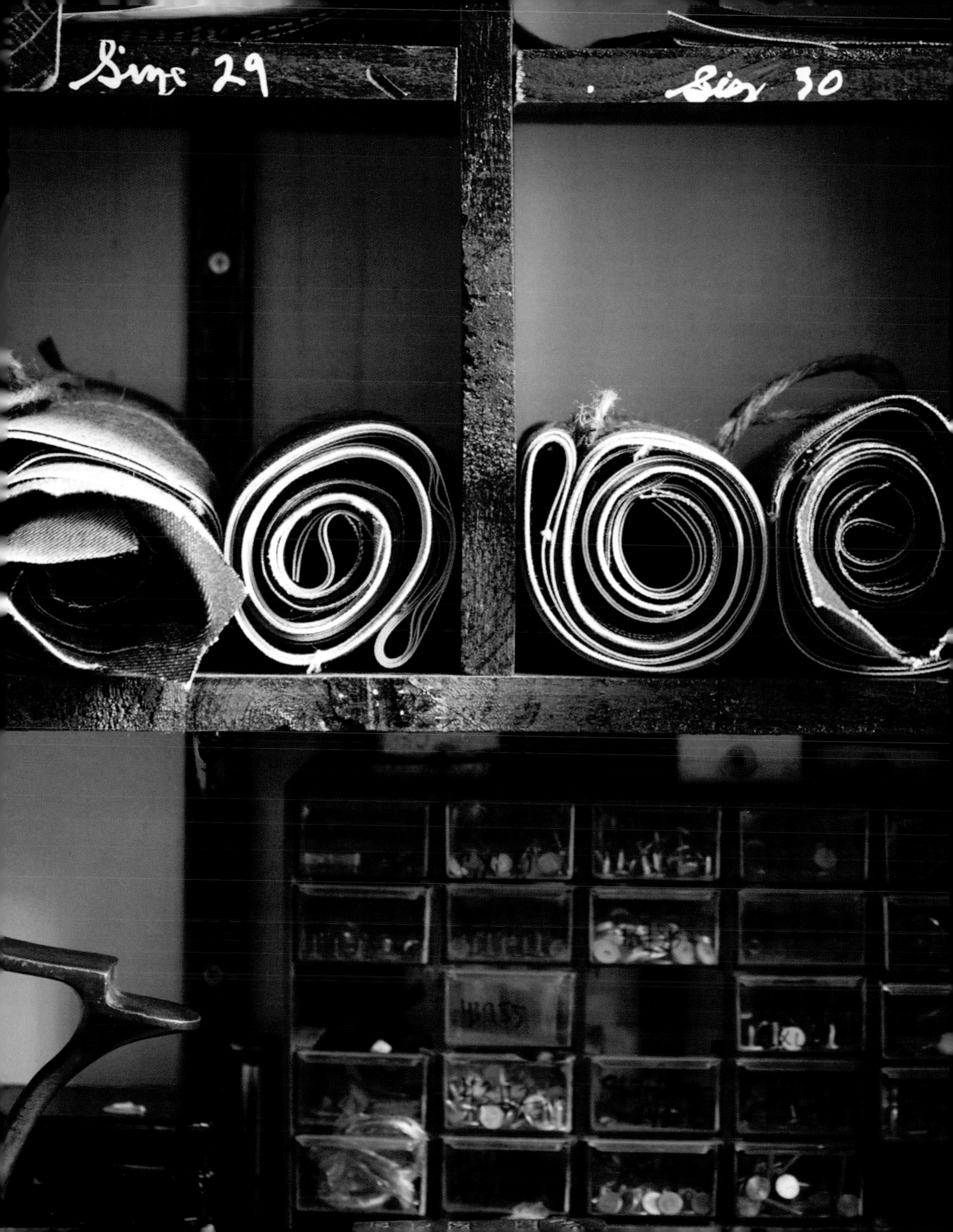
Size 29
Size 30

EMBROIDERY

Bluebell received its name through an employee competition. The brand was previously sold under the name, "Hudson Overall Company" (established in 1914), which was run by brothers C. C. and Homer Hudson. Blue Bell was effectively coined in 1918, when the company began branding their overalls as "Hudson Overall Company's Blue Bell Overalls" in promotional paper items such as flasher tags and advertisements in local periodicals. Bluebell purchased Baltimore brand Casey Jones, which had within its portfolio several other small brands, one of which was Wrangler (first trademarked by Casey Jones Overall Company in 1905). Blue Bell hired famed rodeo tailor Rodeo Ben (also from Baltimore) to lead the prototyping and development of a western line for authentic cowboys. It was initially known as "Blue Bell's Wrangler;" after a while it was named "Blue Bell Wrangler," until finally, "Wrangler." They launched Rodeo Ben's prototypes on rodeo competition cowboys from 1947 to 1949, conducting field testing and refinement of patterns, fabrics, and construction until finally arriving at the standard model for the 11MW and 11MJ in 1949, when it was launched to the general public.

–Evan Morrison, denim consultant

Years before Wrangler existed, Blue Bell had an established department for custom chain stitching for company logos and names. In the late 1940s, Wrangler used embroidery as a way of advertising their brand. Wrangler sponsored rodeo riders, who would wear Wrangler denim, as well as the rodeo clowns, who wore oversized denim pieces. The words "WRANGLER JEANS, SHIRTS JACKETS" were iconically embroidered on the back of the apparel. Using bold colors such as bright yellow with extra large embroidery resulted in an amazing, bold graphic design that is sheer eye candy! It was an advertisement poster and amazing display of craftsmanship on a denim canvas.

This style of embroidering on denim is gaining popularity within boutique denim brands and artisans who personalize denim jackets and shirts. Larger brands are also adding a touch of this heritage branding; DENHAM the Jeanmaker embroiders their name on the inside of the waistband of their jeans. Again we see a more subtle, hidden take on denim branding.

Lee® began making oversized Cowboy Pants for rodeo clowns after launching its Lee® Riders ad campaign in 1946. These "Rodeo Clown Pants," with all the features of the Lee® 101 Rider cowboy pant, were made to be worn with suspenders and became a common sight at American rodeos. Lee®'s earliest rodeo clown pants had "Lee® RIDERS" emblazoned across the front and back in red embroidery. Later, the letters were screen printed.

–Jean Svadlenak, museum consultant, and Lee® Jeans archivist & historian

Lee® Rodeo Clown Pants embroidered with Lee® Riders logo, 1956–1960
Courtesy of Lee® Jeans / Photographer Bobbie Hamzioui

Opposite page:
1950s Blue Bell Wrangler (post-1955) 66MWZ
embroidery jacket, chain stitch detail on back
*Courtesy of Wrangler Archive /
Photographer Joey Seawell*

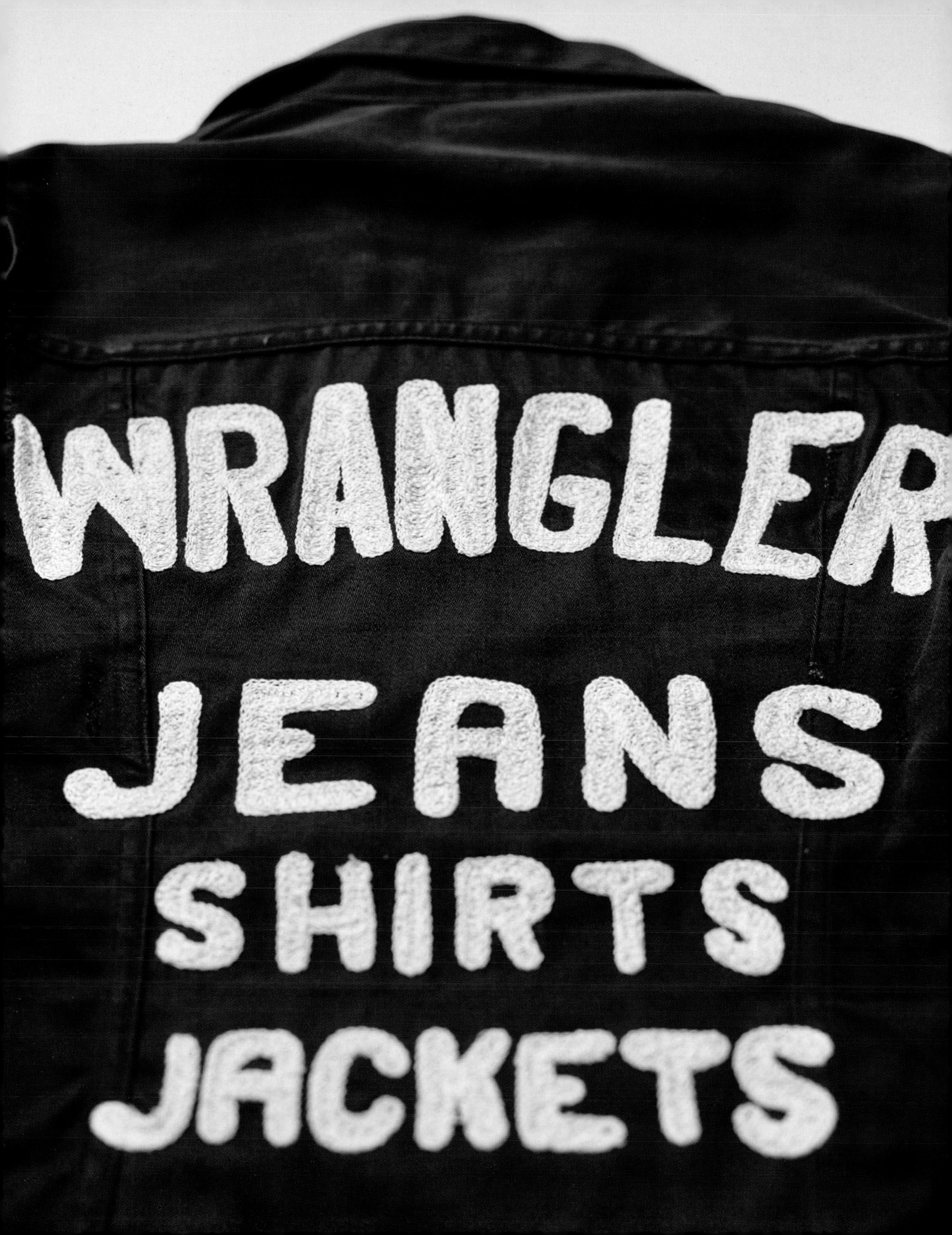
WRANGLER
JEANS
SHIRTS
JACKETS

1950's Blue Bell Wrangler (pre-1955) 12MWZ embroidery jacket chain stitch detail on back
and Blue Bell patch on shoulder
Courtesy of Wrangler Archive / Photographer Joey Seawell

1950s Blue Bell Wrangler (post-1955) 66MWZ embroidery jacket, detail of Blue Bell shoulder patch
Courtesy of Wrangler Archive / Photographer Joey Seawell

1950s Blue Bell coveralls in vat-dyed gray twill, detailing gold chain stitch "The Man From Wrangler"
Courtesy of Wrangler Archive / Photographer Joey Seawell

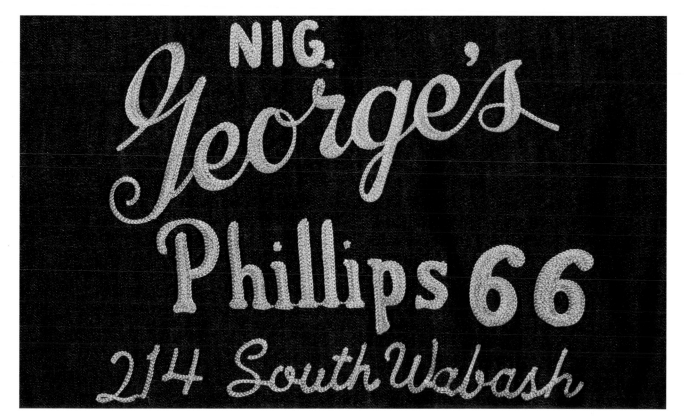

Sugar Cane & Co. emroidery, 2016
Courtesy of Photographer SHUHEI NOMACHI / TOYO Enterprise Co., Ltd.

Diesel product ebroidery, date unknown
Courtesy of Wouter Munnichs, founder of Long John *online magazine*

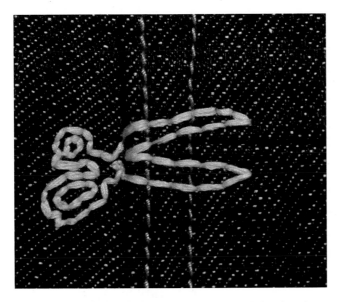

"691 stitches," DENHAM the Jeanmaker chain stitch scissor logo
Courtesy of Ali Kirby & Catharina Veder at
DENHAM the Jeanmaker

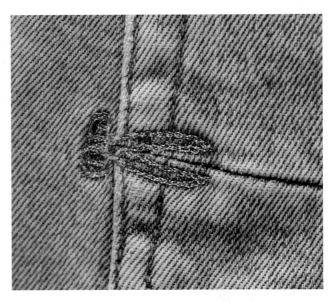

"691 stitches," DENHAM the Jeanmaker chain stitch scissor logo in Italian gold thread
Courtesy of Ali Kirby & Catharina Veder at
DENHAM the Jeanmaker

"691 stitches," DENHAM the Jeanmaker chain stitch scissor logo in Japanese red thread
Courtesy of Ali Kirby & Catharina Veder at
DENHAM the Jeanmaker

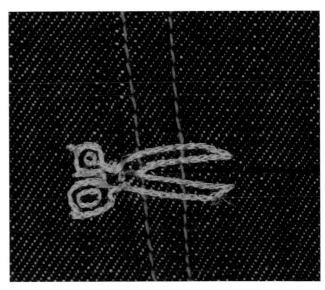

"691 stitches," DENHAM the Jeanmaker chain stitch scissor logo
Courtesy of Ali Kirby & Catharina Veder at
DENHAM the Jeanmaker

DENHAM the Jeanmaker chain stitch logo on inside waistband
Courtesy of Ali Kirby & Catharina Veder at DENHAM the Jeanmaker

"'W,' which stands for the Works; that's what Iron Heart comes under in Japan. It can also be an 'M' for motorcycle. I believe it also [looks like] a very crude engine of a motorcycle, too. It's used to replace a bike engine in some of our branding." –Sam Poole
Courtesy of Sam Poole of Iron Heart International Ltd.

Kings of Indigo hidden back pocket embroidery, c. 2017
Courtesy of Kings of Indigo

Direct-to-garment chain stitch embroidery done on a Singer 114w103 Vintage Lee® Rider, Made in USA
By Brian Blakely, Queens, New York, Courtesy of Blakely Custom Embroidery

Direct-to-garment chain stitch embroidery done on a Singer 114w103 Vintage Lee® Rider, Made in USA
By Brian Blakely, Queens, New York, Courtesy of Blakely Custom Embroidery

I started doing embroidery about two and a half years ago now, while I was working at Knickerbocker Manufacturing. When I first started on the machine, I had no intentions of falling in love with it as I did. My goal was to write my name on a jacket I owned. Something about it though, the machine, the way the gears spin, and the foot clacks up and down, it hooks you.

My favorite pieces generally aren't the elaborate ones or the largest-scaled pieces even. I catch myself loving a good filled-in script or some block letters more than anything generally, when you're able to see a design, the pattern of the stitch, and how you lay it down, not only the image it creates as a whole.

–Brian Blakely, Queens, New York, Blakely Custom Embroidery

MARKETING

From early Levi Strauss & Co. counter cards, point-of-sale signs, banners, promotional giveaways, and packaging to modern-day advertising, marketing has been one of the most important ways for a denim brand to tell its story. Mascots have also been created to entice and sometimes capture the spirit and heart of a denim brand. One of the most iconic is the Buddy Lee® doll. In 1920, H. D. Lee® salesman Chester Reynolds started sourcing for a doll to wear the mini promotional overalls that the company handed out at county fairs. Doll found, Reynolds arranged for several overall-clad dolls to be placed in the window display of Dayton's department store in Minneapolis. The sales force agreed to have special dolls produced, and Buddy introduced each new Lee® product for the next forty years. Famous denim-clad Buddy dolls include the Cowboy, Engineer, and Farmer.

While visiting Cone Mills I heard two great marketing stories. The first was how the Pinto Wash denim was born from a natural disaster and was cleverly spun (pun intended) into a marketing phenomenon (see page 242). The second was how Levi's® Vintage Clothing took a small amount of Cone deadstock denim and created the 501® Mirror Jean (see page 254).

World War II-era counter card
Courtesy of Levi Strauss & Co. Archives

Counter card, c. 1950s
Courtesy of Levi Strauss & Co. Archives

Counter card, c. 1950s
Courtesy of Levi Strauss & Co. Archives

Levi Strauss & Co. advertising sign
Courtesy of www.sonofastag.com

Opposite page:
Levi Strauss & Co. check blotters, used to blot
ink from a fountain pen; a gift with purchase
Author's collection / Photographer Joey Seawell

215

Buddy Lee® doll wearing Lee® Cowboy Pants, 1949–1960
Courtesy of Lee® Jeans / Photographer Bobbie Hamzioui

MARKETING

Buddy Lee® doll wearing Lee® overalls, shirt, and cap, 1949–1960
*Courtesy of Lee® Jeans /
Photographer Bobbie Hamzioui*

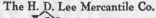

Lee® print advertisement for Lee® Union-Alls, 1919
Courtesy of Lee® Jeans

Lee® print advertisement for Lee® Cowboy Pants, 1941
Courtesy of Lee® Jeans

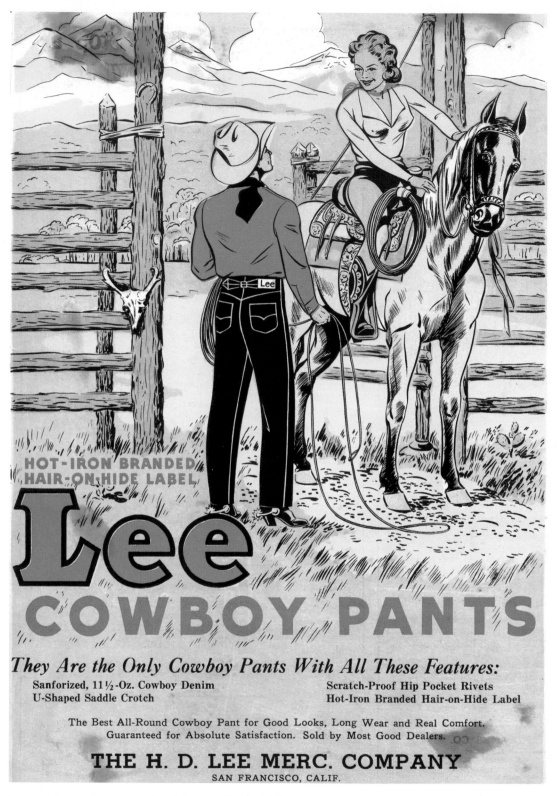

Lee® print advertisement for Lee® Cowboy Pants, 1941
Courtesy of Lee® Jeans

220

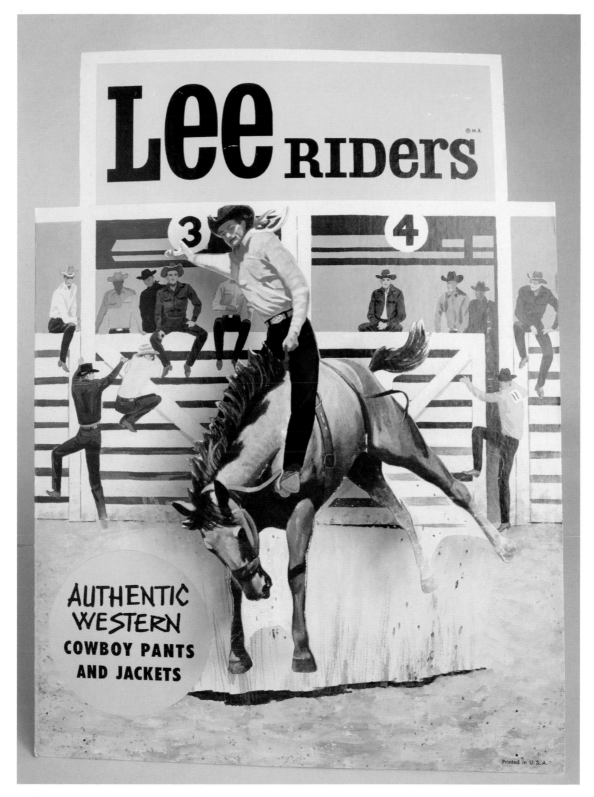

Lee® point of purchase sign for Lee® Riders, c. 1960
Courtesy of Lee® Jeans / Photographer Bobbie Hamzioui

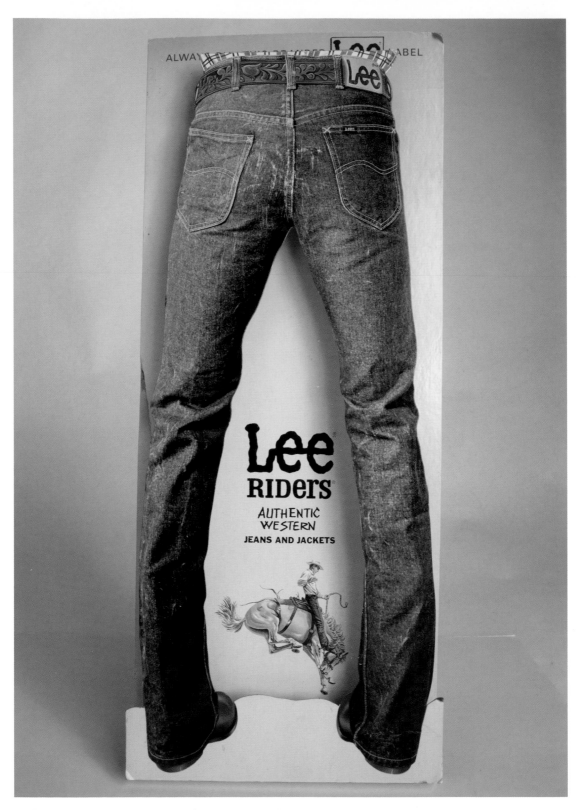

Lee® point-of-purchase sign for Lee® Riders, c. 1986
Courtesy of Lee® Jeans / Photographer Bobbie Hamzioui

Lee® point of purchase sign for Lee® Riders for Kids, c. 1950
Courtesy of Lee® Jeans / Photographer Bobbie Hamzioui

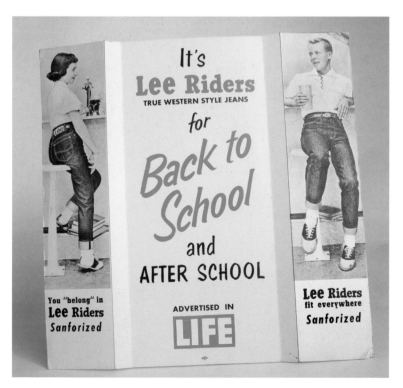

Lee® back-to-school point-of-purchase sign for Lee® Riders, c. 1950
Courtesy of Lee® Jeans / Photographer Bobbie Hamzioui

Lee® print advertisement for Lee® Cowboy Pants, 1944
Courtesy of Lee® Jeans

Lee® print advertisement for Lee® Cowboy Pants, 1946
Courtesy of Lee® Jeans

Lee® giveaway for Lee® Riders, 1950
Courtesy of Lee® Jeans

Lee® print advertisement for Lee® workwear, 1950
Courtesy of Lee® Jeans

Lee® print advertisement for Lee® workwear, 1943
Courtesy of Lee® Jeans

Wrangler promotional items from 1960s to 1990s
Courtesy of Wrangler Archive / Photographer Joey Seawell

Wrangler promotional items and denim-covered items from 1960s to 1990s
Courtesy of Wrangler Archive / Photographer Joey Seawell

Opposite page:
Blue Bell Wrangler products, promotional items,
denim-advertising banner, and packaging from 1950s
*Courtesy of Wrangler Archive /
Photographer Joey Seawell*

1950s Blue Bell Wrangler box top from 888MJB men's jacket featuring famous cowboys who endorse Wrangler and 1952 cowboy rodeo artwork by Fred Ludekens
Courtesy of Wrangler Archive / Photographer Joey Seawell

Wrangler-izing America means making every man, woman and child in America conscious of the Wrangler brand and what it stands for: Quality, Fashion, Value, Guarantee.
Wrangler-izing America means making America aware of our credo: "Wrangler thinks Americans spend too much for clothes. (And we're doing something about it.)" This year, the only thing silent about Wrangler will be the "W."

1970s Wrangler promotional matchbook
Courtesy of Wrangler Archive / Photographer Joey Seawell

1970s Wrangler brass belt buckle featuring Bucking Bronco Wrangler logo
Courtesy of Wrangler Archive / Photographer Joey Seawell

1960s Wrangler fast-color rope logo bandanas
Courtesy of Wrangler Archive / Photographer Joey Seawell

Early 2000s Blue Bell Wrangler reproduction denim banner with co-branded logo
Courtesy of Wrangler Archive / Photographer Joey Seawell

1980s Wrangler Bucking Bronco denim banners in large and small sizes
Courtesy of Wrangler Archive / Photographer Joey Seawell

1950s (pre-1955) sample denim banner for promotion of Blue Bell Wrangler western clothing, including cartoon similar to qualitag books
Courtesy of Wrangler Archive / Photographer Joey Seawell

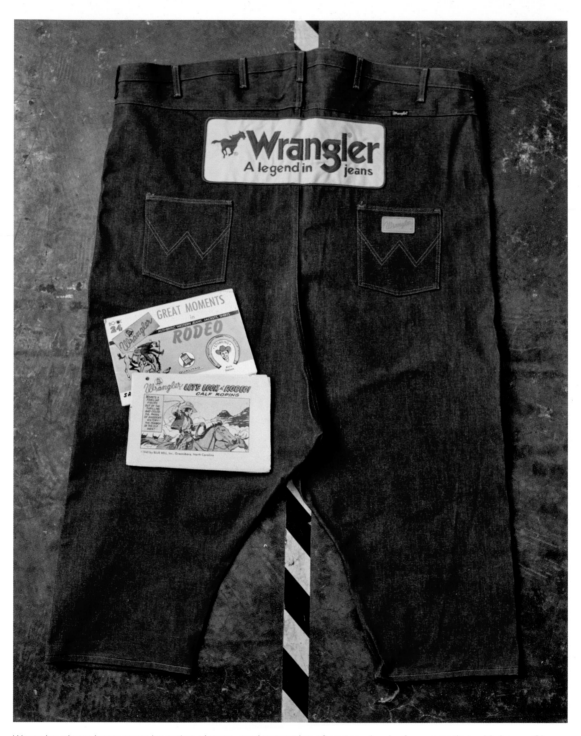

Wrangler clown jeans worn by rodeo clowns, and examples of cartoon books for promotion with jeans. Clown pants from 1980s, noting the Dale Earnhardt-era branding, booklets from 1950s/60s.
Courtesy of Wrangler Archive / Photographer Joey Seawell

1930s Casey Jones work dungarees with UFO rivets, cinch buckle, arcuate stitch, and co-branded cloth label with Cone Deeptone denim 8 oz., complemented by paper handout from a retailer selling Casey Jones overalls
Courtesy of the Morrison Collection / Photographer Joey Seawell

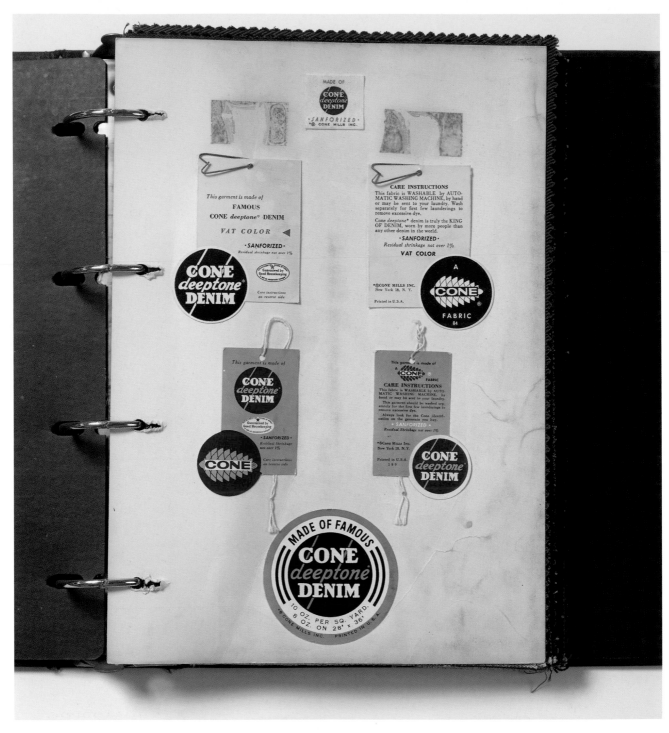

Cone Deeptone denim labels from Cone Mill archive
Courtesy of Cone Denim LLC, a division of International Textile Group

MARKETING

Deeptone ad: Cone Mills Archive
Courtesy of Cone Denim LLC, a division of International Textile Group.

Deeptone ad: "Pop, who put the deeptone into denim?" Cone Mills Archive
Courtesy of Cone Denim LLC, a division of International Textile Group.

MODERNIZING
AN ANCIENT STAPLE

I F A PLAN to modernize the principal work clothing fabric had been proposed prior to the introduction of CONE *deeptone* DENIM, it would have been received with amazement. The qualities and appearance of denims were considered about as fixed and immutable as an oak tree. Apparently the old rather dirty and dusty looking cloth was going to be with us forever.

Fortunately there were those in the industry who thought otherwise. They realized that no fabric can endure if it does not conform to contemporary needs and contemporary tastes. The new Deeptone Blue and the tough Leathery Finish were announced on April 24, 1936. If a history of the work clothing business is ever written, this will certainly become an important date.

The adoption of the new cloth was effected with the minimum of dislocation among manufacturers, by the simple but important expedient of withholding the announcement until producers were cutting the new cloth and had largely disposed of the old.

Modernization of merchandising methods went hand in hand with modernization of the fabric. *The Denim Book* was published to focus attention on the importance of overalls to the retailer and to explain how denim garments should be bought, displayed, promoted and advertised. Soon distributors and producers began to realize that an entirely new kind of advertising had been evolved to meet the new conditions. For Cone advertising of denims has not followed the usual procedure. It has rather endeavored to reach the consumer through the manufacturer or wholesaler, and it has worked out a new technique of promoting the different brand names jointly with the denim. An industry-wide point of view has prevailed and a consistent attempt has been made to win for the entire overall business a high place in the consumer's esteem and a more equitable share of the consumer's dollar.

Page from a Cone Export & Commission Co. half-century book, 1891–1941; copyright 1941
Courtesy of Cone Denim LLC, a division of International Textile Group.

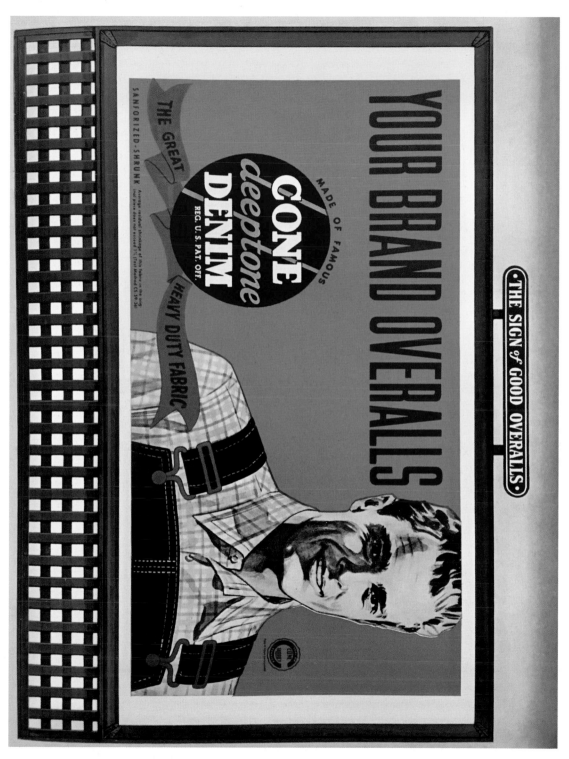

Page from a Cone Export & Commission Co. half-century book, 1891–1941; copyright 1941
Courtesy of Cone Denim LLC, a division of International Textile Group.

The Story of the First Bleached Jeans

On June 15, 1969, downtown Greensboro was hit with a downpour of six inches in a twenty-four-hour period. **The Greensboro Daily News** *reported that Cone Mills was the industry hit hardest by the deluge. As a result of flooding at the White Oak Plant, millions of yards of denim stored in the warehouse were soaked with water, and high school students were hired to help wash and dry the fabric to keep it from mildewing.*

To Cone officials, this seemed like a catastrophe. But, a young denim merchandiser in New York's Cone Marketing Division heard what had happened and suggested that the White Oak Plant run the fabric through a solution to randomly remove the dye and give the denim a faded, mottled appearance.

An advertisement for the denim ran in **the Daily News Record** *and over 50,000 designers, manufacturers, and retailers rushed to place their orders. After the denim was made into garments, thousands of college campuses fell in love with it. Pinto wash denim became a rousing success!*

> –Cone Denim LLC, a division of
> International Textile Group.

Pinto Wash print advertisement
Courtesy of Cone Denim LLC, a division of International Textile Group

1960s Wrangler Pinto denim jeans: A 1969 hurricane that flooded the storage units at Cone Mills' printworks facility led to the creation of this bleaching process and a fashion movement favoring acid wash and cloth mutilation trends.
Courtesy of Wrangler Archive / Photographer Joey Seawell

1906 lithograph header ticket label from White Oak Cotton Mills used in shipments of bolts of denim accompanied by a footer label denoting color, grade, width, and weight of cloth
Courtesy of the Morrison Collection / Photographer Joey Seawell

1920s Hamilton Carhartt union-made railroader kerchief illustrated with bust of Hamilton Carhartt, facts about their clothing production, and their original logo, a street "car" set in front of a "heart." Carhartt marketed their brand well with their car and heart emblem, as well as taglines such as "union made with love" and "unionized labor's best friend."
Courtesy of the Morrison Collection / Photographer Joey Seawell

Advertising banner, c. 1900
Courtesy of the Carhartt Archive

N OTE this odd picture of a Car and a Heart. This Trade-Mark for more than a quarter of a century has stood for the highest quality and the greatest value in overalls.

A fac-simile of this Trade-Mark is placed on every genuine CARHARTT. Beware of imitations.

Registered United States Patent Office. All rights reserved. Infringers will be prosecuted to the full extent of the law.

FROM MILLS TO MILLIONS
Carhartt's
CARHARTT OVERALLS
TRADE MARK
ECCE SIGNUM

FIG. 5

FIG. 6

Carhartt Master Cloth

F IGURE 5 is an actual photograph of the under side of a sample of ordinary denim used in manufacturing most brands of overalls. Compare it with figure 6, showing the famous CARHARTT master cloth from which CARHARTT overalls are made. Note the finer, closer, and more accurate weave made possible by the careful selection of the best long-fibre upland cotton grown on CARHARTT cotton plantations and woven in the CARHARTT cotton mills as a further surety of quality. Ordinary denim, while it may feel heavy, usually is "loaded" with starch or other material for "filling" or "sizing"; which washes out the first time to the laundry, leaving the fabric much lighter in weight and greatly shrunk, whereas the CARHARTT master cloth is clean cotton and genuine Indigo dye, and when it goes to the laundry it stands the test. That is one of several reasons why CARHARTT overalls wear longer and shrink less.

FIG. 3

WIDE SUSPENDERS EASY ON SHOULDERS

HEAVY BRASS BUCKLES AND LOOPS

PATENT OVAL BIB WITH HEAVY FOUR-PLY HEM

PATENT SUSPENDERS

ALL POCKET CORNERS GIANT BAR TACKED

CONTINUOUS 4 PLY HEM REINFORCING BIB SEAM

PATENT SIDE FACING PREVENTS RIPS

ROOMY SEAT

FULL CUT LEGS

WIDE LEGS EASILY PULLED OVER SHOES

FIG. 4

WIDE HAND-MADE COAT FACING

PATENT CUTAWAY COLLAR

ROOMY ACROSS SHOULDERS

DEEP CUFF

Carhartt print advertisement, c. 1925, featuring overalls and coat breakdown
Courtesy of the Carhartt Archive

Dad wore 'em, Grandad wore 'em and they're *TOPS* with me!

Carhartt's

● Three generations of the Carhartt family have produced better wearing work clothes for sixty-four years—an outstanding testimonial to the in-built quality, fine workmanship and consistent popularity of our Master Cloth Overalls.

This reputation is just as jealously guarded today as it has ever been—not by producing the most—but the best work garments experience can build—or money buy. We mean it!

You get the roomy comfort, the easy fit, the skilled tailoring and long wearing qualities which insure that top value and bed rock economy. Every Carhartt garment carries the same iron-clad money back guarantee—either our work clothes "make good"—or we do!

You'll find Carhartt's broader selection matching every job need . . . Blue denims, lace back dungarees, famous 11 oz. extra heavy Brown Ducks, dairymen's white drill, waist type overalls, work caps, shop coats and those all-time favorite Western blue jean Round-Up Pants and Western Jackets to match for youngsters. Wear a pair and feel the difference.

The Farmer's Favorite For 64 Years

Here's the new Carhartt Halsey style cap—washable, comfortable, smart looking—economical. Ideal for work, sports or play. In tan chino cloth—or gray.

HAMILTON CARHARTT OVERALL CO.
Detroit 16, Mich.
Carhatt Park, Irvine, Ky.   Atlanta, Ga.   Dallas, Texas

STILL MADE BY THE FAMILY THAT ORIGINATED THEM IN 1889

Carhartt

LOOK FOR THE CAR IN THE HEART!   THE MOST FAMOUS NAME IN WORK CLOTHES

Carhartt **ROUND-UP PANTS** *are sure Tops!*

● These Western Style blue jeans made from famous Carhartt Master Cloth 11 oz. blue denim are <u>Sanforized</u>. They're copper riveted, have zipper flys, are lock-stitched for tough, rough wear—are just the ticket for guys and gals who want that smart, snug-fitting, breezy, easy, cowboy look. Demand Round-Ups by Carhartt for top value.

FOR 63 YEARS THE FINEST WORK CLOTHES MONEY CAN BUY
Carhartt overalls and work garments —with work caps to match—have been honor-built by three generations of the Carhartt family . . . your assurance of lasting quality and value.

CARHARTT OVERALL COMPANY
Detroit 16, Mich.   Carhartt Park, Irvine, Ky.   Atlanta, Ga.   Dallas, Tex.

STILL MADE BY THE FAMILY THAT ORIGINATED THEM IN 1889

Carhartt

LOOK FOR THE CAR IN THE HEART!   THE MOST FAMOUS NAME IN WORK CLOTHES

Carhartt print advertisements, c. 1955
Courtesy of the Carhartt Archive

248

19-features flyer
Courtesy of the Carhartt Archive

Carhartt neon sign
Courtesy of the Carhartt Archive

Carhartt print advertisement with 19-features poster, 1925
Courtesy of the Carhartt Archive

Box packaging for Dawson denim apron
Courtesy of Dawson Denim

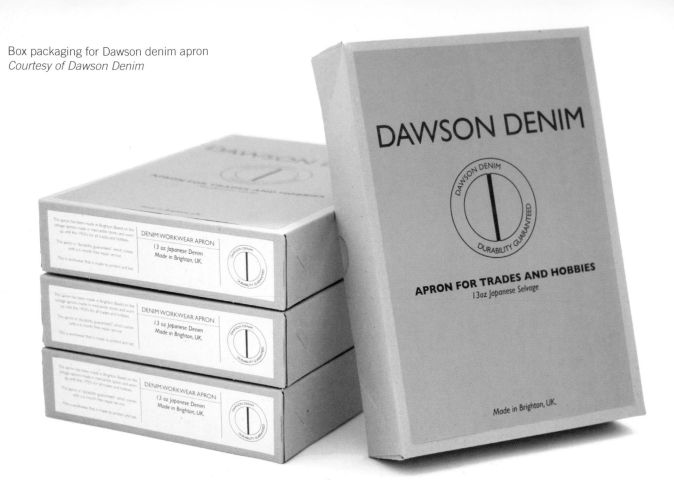

Dawson Denim collaborated with Dry British, Sheffield-based illustrator and signwriter, on this screen-printed collectible felt pennant.
Courtesy of Dawson Denim

MARKETING

DENHAM 10-year anniversary Candiani "Golden Selvedge" jean with Willy Wonka Golden Ticket prize inside, 2018
Courtesy Ali Kirby & Catharina Veder at DENHAM the Jeanmaker

DENHAM 10-year anniversary "Made in Japan" jean delivered with furoshiki wrapping cloth in Katagami stencil print, 2018
Courtesy of Ali Kirby & Catharina Veder at DENHAM the Jeanmaker

251

Left Field custom coal miner printed bandanna
Courtesy of Christian McCann, Left Field NYC

MARKETING

Lee® Riders advertising sign
Courtesy of www.sonofastag.com

Branding details from 1976 501® Mirror Jean for Spring/Summer 2017
Courtesy of Levi's® Vintage Clothing

This jean came about when we were given a small amount of deadstock 1970s denim from Cone Mills. We were really excited at the prospect of making 501®s from original '70s Cone Mills denim.

When we received the fabric we noticed it was left-hand twill, meaning the distinctive grooves in the denim run left to right diagonally down the face of the material. Traditionally Levi's® uses only right-hand twill—especially on the 501®. We figured that the only way we could use this beautiful fabric was if we mirrored every detail of the garment, so when held up to a mirror, it would appear to be a regular right-hand twill 501® Jean.

We mirrored absolutely everything from construction details to the writing that appears on the inside of the rivets. Just a handful of these were made from the deadstock fabric; however, it inspired us to reproduce our 1970s denim in left-hand twill with Cone Mills and make a small run of the 1976 501® Mirror Jean for Spring/Summer 2017.

–Paul O'Neill, head designer
Levi's® Vintage Clothing.

254

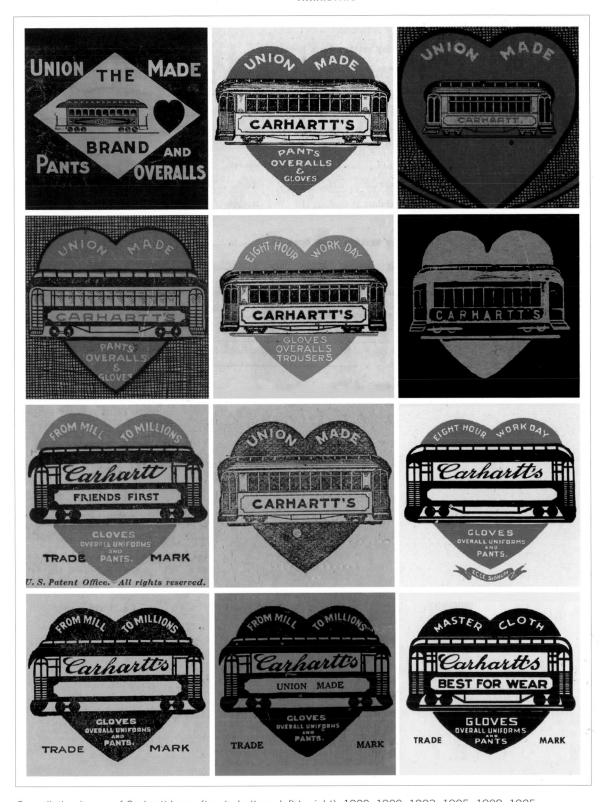

Compilation image of Carhartt logos (top to bottom, left to right): 1900, 1900, 1903, 1905, 1908, 1925, 1913, 1905, 1922, 1925, 1929, and 1951
Courtesy of the Carhartt Archive

Carhartt tin sign
Courtesy of www.sonofastag.com

Headlight tin sign
Courtesy of www.sonofastag.com

Free Land tin sign
Courtesy of www.sonofastag.com

Sweet Orr tin signs
Courtesy of www.sonofastag.com

Sweet Orr advertising sign, c. 1880: Sweet-Orr was founded in Wappingers Falls, New York, by an Irish immigrant, James A. Orr, and his nephews, Clayton E. and Clinton W. Sweet, in 1871. The *New York Times* has said that Sweet-Orr "may actually have been the first commercial jeans producer." *Courtesy of www.sonofastag.com*

Fall/Winter '92/'93 Old Glory catalog
Courtesy of Diesel

Diesel "Old Glory" is Air Freighted!
All Supplies are Strictly Limited
Transportation is Extremely Costly

Nomad (homewashed)

Nomad

Goldigger

Fall/Winter '92/'93 Old Glory catalog
Courtesy of Diesel

Spring/Summer 1993 Old Glory catalog
Courtesy of Diesel

Spring / Summer 1993 Old Glory catalog
Courtesy of Diesel

ACKNOWLEDGMENTS

Andrew Olah & Emily Olah, Erin Barajas, Vivian Wang,
Tracey Panek,
Nancy White, Jean Svadlenak,
Bobbie Hamzioui,
Kris Dumon, Amy Leverton,
Bob Rijnders, Dave J. Moore, Kara Nicholas, Mary Black,
Delores Sides, Kelly Dawson, Scott Ogden,
Jason Denham, Ali Kirby, Catharina Veder,
Elena Piccinni, Marco Montemaggi, Rob & Keith at Eat Dust,
Mohsin Sajid, Karen Chan, Sammy Lau,
Giles Padmore, Sam Poole, Shinichi Haraki, Kyle Stewart, Roosje Kay van Veen,
   Tony Tonnaer, Khoi Thai, Christian McCann, Shane Cullen, Paul O'Neill, Mark Westmorland,
   Karl Thoennessen, Caroline Rice, David Greear, April Spiegel, Linda Rieswick, Rudy
   Budhdeo, Alex Natt, Asako Komatsu, Tomokazu Tanaka,
Craig Errington, Yuri Moreira, Larry Dyne,
Wouter Munnichs, Denver Berman-Jacob, Brandon White,
Brian Blakely, Loren Cronk, Martin Scott Powell, Jonathan Kirby, Brandon Lancaster,
James Richards, Harm Magis, and Jon Daniel

Thanks to Evan Morrison

Evan is an apparel designer, creative director, and vintage-work-clothing expert based in Greensboro, North Carolina. His breadth of knowledge regarding vintage denim, vintage work clothing, industrial apparel and textile manufacturing, and historic overall companies has served as the foundation for the aesthetic of his brick-and-mortar retail store, Hudson's Hill, and his clothing brand, Proximity Manufacturing Company, and for the purpose of consulting with other brands. Since 2015, Evan has worked with Greensboro-based Wrangler (VF Corporation), with the task to consult on the history of the brand, build out the Wrangler Archive, and act as a consulting historian for their participation in *Denim Branded*. He is currently writing a book on the patent history of overalls.

Joey Seawell is an American photographer with a specific interest in love and energy among people in everyday life. His work spans from studio fashion and portraiture to traveling off the beaten path in search of that golden light over a rapidly developing landscape.

His strong interest in details and fine craftsmanship led him to the textile world and more specifically the denim world, where it's all about the little things. www.joeyseawell.com

Nick has more than twenty-five years of experience in graphics and textile design working for major brands in New York and London, such as Levi's (head of graphics Europe, Middle East, and Africa), Puma (head of graphics worldwide), and Nautica. Nick and his wife, Jenny, run the graphic design studio 4th Avenue Graphics (www.4th-avenue.com), specializing in graphics for apparel. With all the experience that Nick has obtained throughout the years in graphic design, denim branding is by far Nick's favorite area. His passion for denim branding has opened up many doors that have enabled him to share his knowledge. Nick lectures at trade events such as Kingpins and at fashion and design institutes, including the Jean School, Denim City, and Strohacker Design School. Nick also consults on denim branding and has written articles on the history and evolution of denim branding for WGSN.

www.denimbranded.com
Instagram: @denimbranded
Facebook: denim branded